D0937597

LOVE LESSONS FOR MY SISTERS

LOVE LESSONS FOR MY SISTERS

◆

HOW TO FIND AND KEEP ALL THE LOVE YOU DESERVE!

Natasha Munson Author of Spiritual Lessons for My Sisters

iUniverse, Inc.
New York Bloomington Shanghai

LOVE LESSONS FOR MY SISTERS
HOW TO FIND AND KEEP ALL THE LOVE YOU DESERVE!

Copyright © 2008 by Natasha Munson

All rights reserved. No part of this book may be used or reproduced by any means, graphic, electronic, or mechanical, including photocopying, recording, taping or by any information storage retrieval system without the written permission of the publisher except in the case of brief quotations embodied in critical articles and reviews.

iUniverse books may be ordered through booksellers or by contacting:

iUniverse
1663 Liberty Drive
Bloomington, IN 47403
www.iuniverse.com
1-800-Authors (1-800-288-4677)

Because of the dynamic nature of the Internet, any Web addresses or links contained in this book may have changed since publication and may no longer be valid.

The views expressed in this work are solely those of the author and do not necessarily reflect the views of the publisher, and the publisher hereby disclaims any responsibility for them.

ISBN: 978-0-595-50488-6 (pbk)
ISBN: 978-0-595-61532-2 (ebk)

Printed in the United States of America

Contents

CENTRAL ARKANSAS LIBRARY SYSTEM
SUE COWAN WILLIAMS BRANCH
LITTLE ROCK, ARKANSAS

Step Three—Expect What You Want

CENTRAL ARKANSAS LIBRARY SYSTEM
SUE COWAN WILLIAMS BRANCH
LITTLE ROCK, ARKANSAS

Step Four—Let Your Intuition Guide You

Step Five—Allow Your Love to Change The World

"To fly as fast as thought
To be anywhere there is
You must first begin by knowing
That you have already arrived."

—Jonathan Livingston Seagull

I have talked to so many women and men that have asked me, sometimes with tears in their eyes, how they can learn to love themselves. In the beginning I was amazed as I looked into the faces of these attractive, sincere people. I just wanted to hug them all and tell them that there was no golden road to love of self I could steer them toward.

I cannot instantly help you to love yourself. All I can tell you and share with you is how it feels to love yourself. The love we have for ourselves will never be surpassed. No one but God will ever love us more than we love ourselves.

One thing I have always had, despite the many dramas I've dealt with in my life, is this undeniable willingness to love myself. And so, one answer I can clearly offer is to look at your life. Look at what you have endured. Look at what you have experienced. And then realize that even though you may have survived the most difficult experiences, and you may have had your self-esteem lowered, your spirit is still seeking to connect with you. Your divine spirit is nearly screaming at you that you deserve love. How do I know this? Because you're reading this book. You are inquiring about love.

I know our spirits seek out the information we need when we are ready to receive that information. So as simple as it may sound, I want you to embrace one message: You are ready for love. You are absolutely ready.

Now all you have to do is take time to appreciate you. Take the time to appreciate every emotion you have experienced, every lesson you have learned, and every relationship you have been a part of. Take the time to honor the person you are right now. Give yourself credit for still believing in and wanting love. Recognize that no matter how much you have endured you still want to feel love. That is the beauty of the human spirit. We all want love. We all deserve love.

I often look back at those beautiful, intelligent people who ask me with such sincerity how I learned to love myself and I smile and say, "I never stopped loving myself. I just needed to be reminded of the great spirit that I am."

So this book is a gift of love from me to you, to remind you of the great spirit that you are and to guide you toward loving you. You already have love inside of you—you just need to honor it, accept it, and give it to yourself.

Live a Life You Love!

Natasha Munson
www.sisterlessons.com

In/Sane

1 out of 4
maybe 7 out of 8
I can't get the statistics straight
but I know it means
my sisters
were touched
and violated
by a friend of yours
that man of yours
that husband of yours
that brother
that uncle
that cousin
that father
of yours
touched a girl in ways
that made her feel
less than
confused
violated

petrified

I know it means
only a few women
went unscathed
only a few women survived
without being touched
in their private places
only a few women had the chance
to come out sane
the rest of us were left

to cry tears of torment
as we wondered why
and looked for a place
to point the guilt
and lay the burden down
but we never could
get free

Some of us had happy childhoods
free to play and dream
then our worlds were changed

when some stranger off the street
or friend of a friend
or a man we trusted
looked at us with an evil gaze
and changed our life
as we cried, fought, screamed,
begged, pleaded, and prayed
this man turned us
from innocent to survivor
in just one day

How many of us had our lives changed
in just one day
one moment
How many of us can still feel the tears from that day
How many of us left a part of our soul in that moment
How many of us want to reclaim our innocence
learn to trust and love again
free ourselves from the painful memories of the past
and step into a future filled with love

It started with a statistic

1 out of 4
maybe 7 out of 8
I can't get the statistics straight

but I know it means
my sisters
are going to end this tragedy
as strong, beautiful, inspirational women
We will find a way to reclaim
our innocence
our trust
our life
our hope
our peace
our power
our freedom
our love

Step One—Release Your Past & Claim Your Loving Future

○ ○

So many times we hold ourselves back from fully loving others and ourselves because we have not clearly examined our heart. So many of us have endured abuse in some form that has scarred our heart and made us wary of falling for love. Sometimes we have had moments in our life that have altered our ability to love unconditionally. And so, before we look for love outside of ourselves we are going to begin with you acknowledging your past, releasing your emotional tie to any painful memories, and remembering the lessons that can help you create a life filled with love.

Freedom

My high school sweetheart and I were making out passionately when a flash suddenly went through me. It was like exiting a dark cave and bursting into sunlight, eyes squinting and trying to make out your surroundings. All of a sudden I felt as if I were alone. I tuned out what my boyfriend was doing and focused on the thoughts that had begun to flood my mind.

In flash after flash I saw myself with two ponytails, a puffy yellow coat and a man telling me to follow him or he would kill my parents. I felt violated and I began to squirm. I had to get away from my boyfriend. I started thinking it wasn't right for women to be touched in that way. I instantly equated sex as something only bad people do and something only men enjoy.

The day I remembered my past changed my life. I burst into tears and my sweetheart began wiping my face. Although I knew he was asking me what was wrong, I couldn't hear him. There was no sound. He held me close and I prayed for the moment to pass. I prayed to release all those horrible thoughts from my mind.

But my spirit must have been ready for the truth because the thoughts remained.

As a young woman who has witnessed both physical and emotional abuse, I know fully that your own mind can become your worst enemy and you can begin to blame yourself for the experiences, feel unworthy of love, have your self-esteem lowered, and either express your hurt sexually or withdraw from sexual expression altogether.

During my journey to healing so many of my sister friends shared their experiences with me. More often than not, a woman you know, are close to, laugh and share secrets with has endured some form of physical, verbal or sexual abuse. There are so many of us holding in this secret as if we are the ones that caused the pain and the shame.

Sisters, you are not responsible for what you endured, but you are responsible now. You are responsible for your happiness and mental freedom now. I achieved my own personal freedom when I released myself from all negative feelings based on my childhood. I no longer allowed myself to feel ashamed, embarrassed, disgusted, disappointed, bitter, or angry about those experiences.

One of the most difficult things any woman or man that has experienced abuse can do is forgive the abuser. Our second most difficult step is releasing ourselves from any feelings of blame.

Release the person from any hatred or anger you may have toward him or her. You need to forgive the person for affecting your life in such a traumatic way. Forgiving your abuser really has nothing to do with the abuser. Dr. Martin Luther King, Jr., once said, "He who is devoid of the power to forgive, is devoid of the power to love."

Forgiving your abuser gives you the freedom to love, trust and be released from the pain of the past. So in forgiving yourself and your abuser, you release yourself from the negative feelings and painful memories of the past and move forward as a spiritual being, ready and willing to love without judging others based on your past.

Life cannot be lived well if you have one foot in your past and one foot in your future. In order to move forward, toward a life you love, you have to release the past and step toward your future. I know you will always remember your painful experiences but to find love you must free yourself from living with those memories everyday.

Since we are on this earth we can choose a life of happiness, no matter what we may have endured in our past. In the current moment of our life we can choose to be the epitome of love, happiness and joy or we can allow our painful past to limit our lives, leaving us to be bitter, unhappy and unfulfilled. As an adult, you now have the power to choose and create a life you love.

You deserve all the love, peace, wealth and happiness God can bring into your life and to receive those blessings, you will have to choose to forgive yourself and others.

Forgiveness will give you the freedom and peace of mind you seek.

Lesson
To have love in our lives we must release ourselves from any feelings of anger or hatred and learn to forgive.

Moment of Power

I remember when I first found out that someone close to me was on drugs. I actually received a call from one of my credit card companies. A woman from the company was calling to tell me that they had noticed an unusual surge in my spending. I had never really used the credit card, and in the last couple of days thousands of dollars in charges were now on the account. I sat down in disbelief. I thought perhaps I had lost the card or it had been stolen. I didn't know what was going on.

I sifted through the items in my desk drawer and found my credit card. I told the service rep that I had my card. Her next words seemed to come out syllable by syllable in very slow motion. "Is there anyone else that could have access to your card?" she said. I looked around my office slowly in disbelief.

The only person that had been in there was my boyfriend. I said, "I'm not sure" and swallowed very hard. She told me that they would like to help me in any way. The credit card company realized that I had not been making the charges so I needed to advise them of the next step. I said okay and ended the phone call.

I walked slowly into my bedroom and there, unbelievably, was an empty crack cocaine vial on the carpet. I bent to my knees and the tears fell hard. They turned into sobs and body wrenching tears. All the fears I had held in my subconscious were now out in the open. There was no denying this.

There was no denying my boyfriend's recent mood changes and weight loss. There were times he would stay out longer than expected. There were times when he looked me in my eyes and lied and I knew it. But what do you do when you're a single parent who feels lost, trapped, depressed and scared? Where do you go when the one world that you know, that you created, is now crumbling? What do you do when the truth hits you head on?

That was the last moment of my insanity. That was the last moment of listening to his dreams and fears. That was the last moment of hearing how bad his parents had treated him and how it affected him. This was now personal. My daughter and I were involved. It was time to end the show for myself. Everyone around me knew I was in pain but I had been pretending for years.

I learned so many lessons by going through this situation. Most importantly, I learned to listen to my intuition. I know this is how God talks to us. I learned that we all have to get to know people. We need to take our time with one another. We need to watch the actions of one another. Are your actions in agreement with whom you say you are?

I also learned that anything we attempt to hide from will find us. If we run from the truth, the truth will seek us out. We must live life authentically. We must not hide from who we are or what we are going through.

During that relationship I felt as though I were on an island, all alone, with my pain, misery and depression. But you know, we are never alone. We are never without God, our divine spirit, and our angels. Life can change and get better when you are ready to face what's really going on in your world. Life can only change when you commit to living and walking with your truth. There are many people that can help you get out of the pain if you simply open up to being helped.

Don't live your life in denial. Don't sit and wait for things to change. Don't hope and pray that things will change without taking the necessary steps to make things change.

The minute your life choices hit you hard and you fall to your knees, remember that this is your moment of power. This is the moment that you are acknowledging your life. This is the turning point. Now you are ready to change your life.

What are you going to do now? Are you going to sit with depression until your life ends? Or are you going to get up and make a new way of life? The only thing keeping you down is yourself. All you have to do is get up, live life authentically, make conscious choices, rid yourself and your life of negativity, and believe in the power that exists within you. Even in your lowest moment you are powerful.

Lesson
We all make a choice to allow our life experiences to enrich and empower us, or to leave us feeling bitter and defeated.

If You Don't Stop

In the darkness of day
fists pound away
eating at the spirit
of the helpless victim
     we stand around and cry
little words lead
to fights of thunder
where the walls shake
     we pull up our covers
     and close our eyes
rumblings of mattresses
tossed around
glasses and picture frames
smashed
     we stand at our doors
     and cry
screams of mama
please let me be
screams of we
don't kill my mama

over her sassy words
and independent spirit
where's your spirit gone
as you pound her away
     inner hatred always finds a way
of manifesting itself
but not today
Today we've had enough
Today we're going to put an end to this
and make you go away

Abusers Can Be Scared Too

There was one night that stood out in her memory, the night things changed in her life. For what seemed like hours there were screams, hits, loud thunderous sounds, banging, and what sounded like hell being unleashed.

The young girl had sat upright in her bed the minute the argument began and was well aware of when it hit the escalating point. That night she just could not bare to hear it anymore. She wanted the sounds to stop. She wanted to have a peaceful night of sleep, like any other child.

He didn't hear as she approached. She didn't make a sound as she reached into the drawer and pulled out the object. He never saw her walk closer to him as his fist swung down one more time, pounding and pounding at her mother's face. He only saw the look in her eyes when she stood directly in front of him.

Before he could speak or say a word, it was at his throat. He had brought it back from one of his trips to Africa and she remembered looking at it, smiling, and knowing the machete would definitely stop somebody in their tracks.

His eyes flashed with fear and anger. He tried to speak but the tip of the machete was pointed directly at his throat. She looked him in his eyes and slowly said, "Stop hitting my mother."

He wanted to say something. He wanted to move his neck to look away from her eyes and not feel the pointed tip at his throat. But he couldn't move. His eyes looked uncertain. She pushed it in a little further in case he hadn't heard her that well. "If you ever hit my mother again, I will kill you," she said, looking him in his eyes, removing the machete and walking out of the room.

After that night she would hear him whisper to her mother, who was suddenly his confidant, "That girl is crazy." Suddenly the daughter was the violent one. She laughed at his words. But one thing was certain, he never hit her mother after that. The daughter no longer had to protect her mother from his anger. The night she silently walked into that room was the day all the physical abuse madness stopped and her spirit was heard loud and clear.

I'm not condoning settling violence with violence in anyway. I tell you this to share with you that there comes a point in your life when enough is enough. There comes a time when you become sick and tired, tired and sick, of life being less than you thought it would be. There comes a time when you're fed up with other people stealing your joy and trying to dictate your life. There comes a point in your life when you decide to take control and make the necessary changes.

We all have our moments, our epiphanies; we just need to raise our standards for life. We need to realize that one person can make the difference in the life of another person. One person can help lead another person to happiness.

You can make a difference. Make your life an example. Never let anyone steal your joy or harm your spirit. Never let anyone abuse you in anyway and know that life is what you choose to make it.

Lesson
Life can and will change the moment you decide to take control of it.

Mother Love

I met one of my friends in third grade. My friend and her mom have a relationship that has always been incredible. Their relationship has remained phenomenal throughout the years and has inspired me in so many ways.

I knew, even then, that if I ever became a parent I would be like my friend's mom. Even when she was chastising, she still took the time to listen to her daughter. She always asked about her day and listened to my friend's many rants about life and our childhood and teenage drama. She was there to give advice and always carefully maintained the line of friend and mother.

Now I have several sister friends that have phenomenal relationships with their mothers and I love seeing them interact, listening to how much fun they have together, and how much they know about one another. It's an amazing thing to see.

I know that not all of us are blessed to have such remarkable relationships with our mothers. But somehow, someway, God always provides you with what you need to be inspired. You simply have to be open to seeing the blessings God's giving you. Now my goal is to create the same sense of friendship, love and openness with my daughters as my sister friends have with their mothers.

For those women who have experienced strained relationships with their mothers I would simply offer these words, let it go. Release your mother from your expectations. Release her from the role you wished she would have possessed and acknowledge the person she actually is. She is a human being, just like you. She is not perfect. She had a childhood of her own that may have been filled with pain. Perhaps she did the best she could at the time.

Now it's up to you to create the relationships you want. We must find the relationships that give us hope and focus on those. If you continue to live a life in which you talk about the ways your mother or father disappointed you, you will live a limited life. You will remain emotionally stuck. The only way to have a better relationship with your mother is to release whatever negative feelings you have about or toward her and make peace with yourself.

Just because your mother never hugged you or told you that she loved you, does not mean that you are not worthy of love or a warm embrace. Just because your mother may have uttered words that harmed your spirit does not mean that you are destined to be less than great in this life. Just because your mother did not protect you, love you, support you, embrace you, hug you, get to know you, or cherish you the way you believed she should have, does not mean you are not worthy of these things.

Yes, a mother's words are powerful and affect a child's life. However, it is entirely your decision on how long and whether you allow any negative words or behavior to affect you and your adult relationships.

Lesson
We have the ability to create the relationships we want and deserve.

Worth The Pain

God is always with you. In any moment of your life you are either tuning God in or out. But God is always there to offer love, guidance, support and friendship. The goal of our life is to recognize and appreciate the presence of God in our lives and then share that energy with others. That is our ultimate purpose. But often in life we get thrown off and we wonder what we are supposed to do with our lives. We think that with the state our lives are in God can't possibly be within us.

In my early twenties I went through so much pain and intense struggle. I felt as though I had let God down. Although I was young, I literally felt like an old woman. My steps were slower, my smile was weaker, and my heart was broken. I was so very disappointed in myself. And I felt that because I had made a mistake, or so I thought at the time, that God would never forgive me.

I didn't even think God loved me at that point. I remember sitting and thinking that my life was over. Many times I wished the pain of disappointment could just subside and I could be done with the misery of living on this earth. I never wanted to harm myself but I really wanted the pain to go away.

It seemed as though every day brought another form of misery. I had to withdraw from my college classes because I became pregnant. Family members began to talk about me and put me down. And because I had no money at such a young age I had to walk into an office and ask for financial assistance. With impending motherhood I thought that my life was over. I thought I had to give up on my dreams and that all my dreams would be unattainable.

I eventually learned that becoming a parent does not end your life it expands who you are. If you have love inside, then you are capable of giving more love. If you have a dream you want to obtain, you now have a bigger reason than just your own needs.

Never think that you have to push yourself aside as a priority. The only way to obtain happiness and really love your life is to put yourself first. Parents have to remember and understand that.

When you are happy, you help your child be happy. When you love yourself, you help your child love him or herself. When you pursue your goals, you show your child that the pursuit of dreams is always possible.

As I look back on my life now, I wouldn't change a thing. I appreciate with all my heart, soul and spirit, that God loved me enough to correct my actions and make me a better person.

No matter what we have been through in life it can be turned around for the better. It can be turned around to make us better people and wiser spirits. We really need to stop whining and complaining about the state of our lives and realize that we are blessed every moment that we breathe. We are blessed to be able to talk about the challenges in our lives, because if we trust the process, our talk will soon turn to how we overcame it all.

There is a little saying in the church community, "God is good all the time". All the time.

Believe that.

Lesson
There is always something your spirit can learn from a situation. You must be receptive to the lesson and commit to making better choices so that you can move forward in life.

Stop Punishing Yourself

When I became a parent I thought I was obligated to stay in the relationship with my daughters' father no matter what. I thought that my happiness no longer mattered. I believed that my dreams would have to be put on hold and I would have to endure whatever things the relationship brought to my life. I aged about twenty years because I gave away my power and joy.

I gave away my ability to choose happiness. I foolishly believed that because I had done something that I had not intended (get pregnant without being married) I was being punished. I had let myself down. And I thought I had let God down too.

I was creating my own hell, my own prison. I was punishing myself. I was hurting myself. And the more I retreated into my own world and pushed others away, the more miserable I became. I created a cycle of unhappiness because of my beliefs. I believed that I was no longer able to fulfill my dreams because I now had responsibilities. I believed that even though I was so unhappy, I had to stay in the relationship, because of the sake of my children.

I cried so many times until I finally realized I couldn't take anymore. My spirit fought back and told me that life is not meant to be lived in pain.

I learned that many times we create our own hell because we haven't been shown how to create a life we love. We stay in relationships that are toxic to our spirit and hinder our growth because we feel obligated or somehow comfortable. We allow others to tell us what to do with our lives because we do not have enough confidence in ourselves. We allow the years to slip by without us achieving our goals because we waste time and foolishly think we have more than enough time ahead of us. We pray for a way out of our situations and then never begin the actual tasks to make the changes.

So many people deal with pain and stress and the one thing many of them can say is, "I'm blessed because God got me through." God will continue to get you through your situations. But here's a question, "Do you know God will get you to your glory too?"

The lesson in life is that God is not meant to just get us through the bad times. Our God can take us to the powerful, happy times where we're smiling from our soul, loving our life, laughing and loving who we are and how we are.

God can deliver you from foolish thoughts and painful relationships and take you to love, peace and happiness. You just have to change the way you think and do things. Stop putting yourself down. Stop living a life where you 'just get by, have just enough, just make it through' and start living abundantly.

Lesson
Commit to living a life you love and having everything and everyone in your life serve as a reflection of that.

What Do You Do?

What do you do
when the man of your dreams
is really a nightmare
do you cry and scream
or do you pick up
and say goodbye
do you hold on
because of love
or money
or do you slam the door
and say
kiss my ass
honey
do you smile and pretend that love you are in
when you feel trapped
like a black
at a klan convention
or do you curse
and complain
vowing to get out

if he don't straighten up
his mess
do you leave
do you talk
do you complain
do you cry
do you love yourself
do you try
do you do anything

I shall not shrink because you do not trust your power to rise.

Declare Your Freedom

Have you ever had someone call you up, yell at you for some crazy reason, get on your last nerve, hang up and then call you the next day or week like everything was okay? If you're in certain families, that happens all the time. The question is, "When does it end? When do you hold everyone, including family, accountable for his or her actions?"

There are so many people in the world struggling to get over their childhood. There are so many people that have endured abuse of some kind. The problem is that there are many people that do not talk about their history. So many people bottle up their pain because they are afraid to reveal it or afraid of how the family will respond. So many people allow the pain of their past to sit inside their bodies like a toxic element because they are too afraid to let go.

In order to find freedom, which to me occurs on all levels (spiritual, emotional, financial and physical) you have to acknowledge, claim, release and refresh.

First you must acknowledge whatever you've been through in life and whatever you've done to someone else. You have to acknowledge whether you caused pain or were harmed in some way.

Then you must claim the ability to be healed and released from the experience. No you were not responsible for what happened to you. But are you being responsible now? Are you allowing your pain to hold you back from trusting and loving another person unconditionally? Are you holding onto pain because the truth will hurt someone else?

In order to live a life of happiness you have to speak your truth. You have to release yourself from negative thoughts and energy. You must forgive the person that caused you pain and release yourself from pain and anger.

The best gift I gave myself was forgiving the person that caused me pain and forgiving the bystander that could have prevented it all. I released them from my energy. And then they were left to deal with what they had done. Then they were left to acknowledge the pain they caused. And then you know what? I was free. I was refreshed. I could love more fully. I could smile more and laugh harder.

Once you've gone through all these steps, the next step is the most important. You have to declare your freedom. If someone attempts to steal your joy you must combat him or her with your positive energy. If someone attempts to "bring you down a peg" you must remind yourself of the great steps you have taken. If someone wants to only see you as the person you were in the past, you must claim who you are today and get away from that energy.

When you declare your freedom and choose to authentically be yourself, there are no words or people that can harm you. Once when you become accountable for yourself, you then must help people to be accountable for their lives.

The next time someone calls you with some nonsense, take a deep spiritual breath, and simply ask them the real reason for their call. Most of the time people are hurt and are expressing it in the form of anger. Or they're jealous and don't know how to express it. Or they feel as though you're not spending as much time with them anymore. Whatever it is, it can be revealed without all the drama.

And in the end, there is no reason for you to apologize for what you do with your time or energy. The point to be made is that you will not accept negative energy from "mom, dad, sister, brother, aunt so-and-so, or cousin whoever." Negative energy is simply not acceptable.

Lesson
People instantly know how much drama or negative energy you will tolerate. Therefore you must ensure that your spirit remains in a positive place so that you do not attract negative energy and so people can know that you will not accept any form of negativity.

Chicken Little

Have you noticed that some people like creating drama? They walk around with doom-and-gloom all over their face, as though they're Chicken Little. They are the only ones going through things in life and, oh my goodness the world has fallen on their shoulders. Sometimes you just want to grab them by the shoulders, look them in the eye and tell them to cut that crap out!

If you feel like the weight of the world is on your shoulder that is what you are choosing to experience. Everything we do is a manifestation of what we think and believe. Most of our experiences are based on our expectations. So why don't you choose being happy? Why don't you choose to experience love? Why don't you realize that you are not alone? You are never, ever, alone. I don't care how hopeless or depressed you feel, you are not in this life alone. Take a chance and reach out to someone and they just might help you smile, laugh, or live a better life, even if it's only for a moment.

And before you slip back into Chicken Little mode and say, Well I've been through this and I've been through that, just remember, we're not here on earth to debate our experiences. We have all been through things. We are all on a journey to overcome our issues and learn how to love our lives. The key is to have the courage to get over it and still be able to smile. And still be able to be a good person and have love in your heart. The key is knowing that no matter what you go through in life, you can either come through it broken or you can come through it with renewed energy and strength. It's your choice.

For my sisters that need it, remember this:

I may have been abused, but I still have courage. I may have been assaulted, but I still have strength. I may have been beaten, but I'll never be broken. I may have been hurt, but I still have love. I may have had some hard moments, but I have a beautiful life because God is within me. And no matter what anyone attempts to do to me or say about me, they can never take away the pureness of my spirit. This is my life to love!

Lesson

When you are immersed in pain you must stop the "woe-is-me moment" and simply ask yourself, How long do I plan to stay in this place? You are not being tested on how much pain you can endure. Experience your moment; get the lesson and then MOVE ON with your life.

Thankful Tears

I got down on my knees and cried. I didn't cry because of sorrow. I didn't cry because of pain. I didn't cry for forgiveness or for help with a stressful situation. I got down on my knees and cried so that I could properly thank God for all that he has done in my life.

We need to remember that God always has our best interests in mind. Though we can feel overwhelmed by life, we are always headed in the right direction. God will never let you stray too far once you've welcomed God into your heart.

You will never go through more than you can handle. You will never have more than you can bear. God knows your load. God knows what your spirit can carry. God knows the lessons you need in order to have a strengthened spirit, renewed trust, and believing heart.

So tears were shed in appreciation, and I said thank you. Thank you for delivering me. Thank you for saving me. Thank you for using me as a vessel. Thank you for touching my heart, my spirit and my soul.

As long as we walk with God we will never have to live with stress. There is nothing that God cannot heal or eliminate. Life is only stressful when you don't know how to let go of your problems. Sometimes, you have to exhale and hand it over to God. You are blessed! Be thankful for all that God has done and will do for you.

Lesson
Thank God for every moment of your life.

"There is no difficulty that enough love will not conquer, no disease that enough love will not heal, no door that enough love will not bridge, no wall that enough love will not throw down, no sin that enough love will not redeem ... It makes no difference how deeply seated may be the trouble, how hopeless the outlook, how muddled the tangle, how great the mistake. A sufficient realization of love will dissolve it all. If only you could love enough, you could be the happiest and most powerful being in the world."

—Emmet Fox

Step Two—Create a Foundation for Love

○ ○

Once we have found freedom from our past, we must know that we are worthy of love. The love we have for ourselves must exude through our being and reflect into our lives. To remain balanced in love you must first truly love yourself for the spirit that you are, not for the material things you possess or the beauty of your outer being. You must commit to being the best person you can be and treat yourself with love, respect, and kindness. Honor your heart, time and energy and expect the same qualities in all of your relationships—friendship and intimate.

Speechless

I was out to dinner with a man I had met recently. We were having a great time. We were laughing throughout the conversation and the wine was flowing. Then, he stopped suddenly, looked at me intensely and said, "I have to share something with you."

I sat up anxiously.

"Hmm, I guess I'll just say this because you have every right to know," he added.

My intuition said "uh-oh," but I didn't say anything out loud.

He took a sip of wine and said, "You are a wonderful woman and I can't believe you're in my life."

I sat back and relaxed a little. I thought he was going to say he was married or something.

"And before we go any further," he continued, "I just have to let you know that I have had homosexual experiences."

I almost choked on my wine.

Believing that perhaps I had lost my hearing I said, "What?"

He started to tell me the story. I stopped him in mid-sentence.

"No, no. I heard you. I'm just wishing that I hadn't heard you," I said. Then I sat back, stunned and said, "But thank you for telling me."

He started to tell me his experiences, which involved some childhood trauma, as I did my best Bambi impression and stared at him with a dazed look in my eyes. Well, wasn't this a slap of "Welcome to Atlanta" right in the face? I shook my head and thought, what am I still doing here and why am I listening?"

As the thoughts raced through my head, I finally uttered, "Wait, wait. I don't mean to cut you off. But this … I … I've never had a conversation like this before. My heart and spirit feel crazy. I'm wondering what' s up with my intuition. And you know," I said as I stood up, "I really have to go."

And I left.

So the question that hit as I walked out the door was, how did I attract this?

In my sleep the answer hit me, just like every goodbye ain't gone, every issue isn't dead until your spirit is healed.

This man was denying who he was at the core. He was battling being gay and I was battling being a single mom. I believe we were brought together so that we would both have to acknowledge and accept who we were truly meant to be as individuals and to learn that the key to finding love is to love and honor yourself first—every part of you.

Forgive yourself for all the decisions you have made. Embrace the powerful person you are today. Love the person that you see in the mirror—all of you. Acknowledge the greatness that resides within you. Release yourself from the pain of childhood drama and trauma. Release yourself from having any anger in your being. Free yourself so that you have can have pure, unconditional love for yourself.

Lesson
Accept who you are.

Beauty

it's not the eyeliner
or the lipstick
it's not the sassy walk
or sweet talk
it's about you
on the inside

it's your soul girl
your spirit
these are your strengths
this is where your beauty lies
this is how you define your life

your spirit determines how you look at the world
and at others
do you have compassion
understanding
can you relate?

your spirit tells you

that your beauty
is the beauty of the world
God created everything
to have a purpose
when you know this
you can look at a landscape
and smile and know
as perfect as those trees are
so too are you
      this is peaceful beauty

so don't be misled
don't think that your short skirts
and men wanting you
is what makes you beautiful
beauty is much deeper than that

just as you must respect life
you must respect yourself
that means knowing
that within this massive world
        you are unique
there is no one exactly like you

        yet we are all reflections of God.
hold these thoughts
cherish them
expect more
        and you will get more

don't limit yourself
or the definition of beauty
as someone who dresses up pretty
intelligence is beautiful
creativity is beautiful
love is beautiful
respect is beautiful
individuality is the best

there's nothing wrong with eyeliner
or lipstick
just know
that's not all there is
to beauty
        to You

Does He Have Issues?

As women who are dating for the purpose of finding a loving, committed relationship, we must be careful in our selection process. The lesson I have learned is that it takes time to get to know someone and you must get to know a man during his good and bad moments. It is essential that you see this man around his family, loved ones and friends.

When I began dating, my friends and I created a list of wants. Our lists included what we wanted in a man. I highly recommend that you create your own list as well. It may sound silly but I believe it truly helps you in your relationship decisions. Also visualization, being able to envision what you want in life, truly works. So committing your wants on paper will help you get closer to your dream man.

A few of my dating essentials included a man that has long-lasting friendships. I believe every good man has a friend he's known since grade school or at least for several years. I believe it is essential that a man appreciates his parents and has a loving, communicative relationship with them. Or at least made peace with the type of relationship he does have with his parents.

Every woman should be able to see a man take responsibility for something in his life. Before you ever become intimate or fall in love with outward appearances, make sure you see this man during his moments of disappointment or anger. How does he deal with a frustrating experience? How does he show love? Does he know how to show gratitude? Does he genuinely say thank you or does he take what others do for granted? Does he take care of his body and his home?

Through my dating experiences I learned that it is best to date a man that has been in love or genuinely loved a woman. It is also important to know whether a man trusts himself and how he views women. If you open the discussion correctly you can find out exactly how a man feels about women and relationships.

During one such conversation I learned that a man did not trust women and thought they made foolish choices because of their emotions. His strong feelings toward women stemmed from his mother. He believed his mother foolishly stayed in a relationship with her husband because of her misguided loyalty, and because she wasn't strong enough to leave the relationship. So he viewed his mother, and as a result, all women, as weak, emotional and incapable of making the right decisions for themselves if they believed they loved a man. He seriously and strongly believed these things, and of course, it affected his relationship with me and other women.

How will this man ever have a loving, fulfilling relationship? Until his mindset changes he will never have a loving relationship because he believes love distorts your judgment rather than enhances your life. But how else would I have known his viewpoint on love if I didn't take the time to ask him about his life and love experiences? Sisters, you have to ask the important questions and set your standards. You are not setting a man up to be interviewed and pummel him with question after question. Rather you are taking the time your soul and heart requires to get to know this man and whether he is capable of loving you and worthy of your heart and time.

Also, the man didn't offer all his negative viewpoints on women in one conversation. I began to see how he truly felt about women during the course of a few dates. But believe me when I tell you, I appreciate every day that I got to learn about him and see his true spirit. By taking the time to get to know who he truly was rather than who he said he was, I knew that he was not right for me as a boyfriend or a friend.

So many times women give away their love without making a man earn their love. You are worth getting to know. You are worthy of love. You are worthy of being pursued. Stop giving away your heart so freely. Your body and heart are too precious for you to just give away because someone says the right words. The only way to have a good relationship is to allow yourself to see the man in action and to have a mental list of requirements that you want in a man.

Lesson
The only way to have a good relationship is to know what you want and accept nothing less than the best.

Bitter People

Do you have someone in your family that is bitter and miserable and the rest of the family dismisses their negative behavior by saying, "that's just how she is?" I think there's always one or more of those in families.

Whenever I am in a bad mood I stay to myself rather than share it with my loved ones. I try not to take out any negative energy on those around me—whether family, friends or strangers. Yet there are some people in this world that feel entitled to be negative and bitter. It is their choice to live with a negative attitude. But let's get to the core of the matter. Why are they so bitter and unhappy?

I remember when I first started saying my signature line, *Live a Life You Love!* I was nowhere near living a life I loved. But God I wanted to believe living a life you love was possible. I knew there were people loving and living their life to the fullest and I wanted that type of life. I wanted to shape my life so that I could love every moment of it. So I put my focus on creating that type of life.

I began to do everything in exact opposite of the negative and unfulfilled people around me.

I saw one person constantly arguing or raising her voice with anyone that disagreed with her, so I took more time to listen to other people.

I saw a man look at his wife with such sadness that it was clear he wished he had never stood at the altar with her. His sadness helped me to realize that I have to know why I love someone. I have to know whether I love my man in the good and bad moments. It is essential for me that he and I become the best of friends, and he has to get along well with my loved ones.

I saw a woman who miscarried several times, always prayed for a baby, and then worked so much that her miracle baby was at daycare and grandma's more than she was with her mom. Through this woman I learned to treasure the moments I have with loved ones and be prepared for what I pray for.

I saw a man constantly beat and cheat on his wife. When they finally separated he met a woman that verbally abused him. He taught me the power of karma and treating people as I would want to be treated.

I saw a woman change her religion for a man and lose all joy in her eyes. She taught me to have my own relationship with God. She taught me to never change my values or spiritual core for anyone but God.

I saw a woman that stayed in an unhappy marriage because her mother didn't believe in divorce. I learned that I will never allow anyone to have more control over my life than God and I do. I also learned that in the end my happiness matters more than what friends or family may think about my decisions.

I saw a married woman move closer to her family because her family thought it was the best thing for her. She became financially dependent on them, got divorced, and took years to have a successful relationship and acquire her own home. She taught me the power of stepping out on faith and making your own space in this world. She taught me that in order for a relationship to work there are only two opinions that matter—his and mine.

Through all of these people I learned that many people remain bitter and unhappy because they are afraid to walk away from a bad decision, they've become financially dependent on someone, or life has made them choose a job they hate. And so, all they do is struggle and they don't know how to live life any other way. No one ever told them that they could live a life they love.

I believe we do our children and ourselves a disservice by not creating lives we love. "Live a life you love may sound like a wonderful affirmation. But in essence, it can be our saving grace. When you tell yourself everyday to live a life you love, you will create circumstances to make that a reality.

If you find work you love, then you will not be miserable and bitter about going there everyday. If you find someone you love from your soul and get to know them as your friend and lover, then perhaps you won't regret marrying them five years from now. If you tell your children to live lives they love, then you will empower them to use their talents, inspire them to start businesses, learn to think outside the box and genuinely love themselves.

Lesson
If we are spiritually aware we can learn from the lives of others and use that knowledge to make better choices for ourselves.

Change Your Thinking, Change Your Life

Every day thousands of people verbally say, if the opportunity ever arises I'm going to do such and such. They tell everyone around them just what they would do when and if they were presented with a life changing opportunity. Then one day, subtle or not, an opportunity is presented to the individual. A real chance to change their life in some way is presented.

Most people will not recognize the opportunity. Others may see it as a potential opportunity, but because it may not be perfectly laid out and tell them specifically what to do, they make excuses and come up with elaborate reasons of why they simply cannot take advantage of the opportunity.

Most people are cowards who have a fear of living outside of their box. People are much more at ease talking about what they want to do rather than actually doing what is required to make things happen in their life.

As cowards who are afraid to live our best life we live with a few thoughts.

How will I ever? we say. The positive response is to trust yourself. Trust your ability to make a decision. Trust that God wants the best for you. Trust that if you begin the process and commit to it, that you will receive the help you need to accomplish your goals.

I cannot imagine, we say. Imagination is what will free you to live a better existence. You must become as imaginative as you were as a child, and dream big. As adults we have been conditioned to limit our thinking and bring our dreams down to what society deems as reasonable and realistic. If you intend, on any level, to live a life you love, then you must not be overly concerned with what society deems as reasonable and realistic. You must ask your spirit to guide you to what is realistic for you. Remember that greatness cannot be confined, and when it is withheld, imagination is the thing that will set it free. Imagine your greatness being let loose.

I've wasted my time, we say. Two things—you are what you believe and you are where you want to be. Understand that clearly. If you truly believe on any level that you have wasted your lifetime then you are right. However if you choose to alter your thinking and say, 'I am going to use this moment as a launching point to change my life,' then you will be in a position of power. You will be in a place to take advantage of opportunities. If you know that you want to do something else in your life, or with your talent, then simply choose to create that. Choose to make that your reality. Remember that if you truly want to be somewhere else in life then you must place your focus on attaining that. When your focus shifts, you will stop having analysis paralysis, you will stop making excuses, you will stop letting any aspect of your life block you from living the life of your dreams, and you will go after what you want with all the passion you possess.

I don't have the time, we say. You have time for whatever you choose to have time for. Countless people waste the moments of their lives and go to bed every night wondering why their life hasn't changed for the better. How can your life change if you don't make time for yourself and do what's best for you?

I'm going to do that someday, we say. Why not today? Do you have a written agreement that you're going to be here in five years to do what you're putting off today? Understand that you choose what you do with your life, your time and your energy. If you have a dream to do something then find some way, however small or large, to make it part of your reality today. Do something other than saying "I'm going to," "One day," or "Some day." Change your wording and you'll change your life.

God will let me know when it's my time, we say. God may have been telling you for years that it's your time to change your life, start a business, end a relationship, start a relationship, move, write a book, travel to a foreign country, learn a new language, or whatever it is that your spirit desires. You just may not have been listening and clearly hearing God.

There is a story of a woman whose town was being flooded. She desperately climbed to the roof and held on to the chimney for dear life. A neighbor came by in a boat and offered help. She said, no thank you, the Lord is going to save me. A dog came by and tried to pull her to safety. She shooed the dog away and said, No, the Lord is going to save me. The police came by with a helicopter and offered assistance. She said, No, the Lord is going to save me.

She passed away in the storm and her first question to God was, why didn't you save me? God said, I sent a dog, a helicopter, and a boat. Why didn't you take my help?

So I kindly remind you to take advantage of your life. Let's choose to stop being cowards and start living great lives. God will speak to us through our intuition and tell us what is right or wrong for us, and then we must trust that voice enough to listen and act upon it. You cannot love your life and live with fear. They do not peacefully coexist. So you must learn to take whatever fear you are feeling and use it to your advantage. Use your fear to take you from coward to glorious. Use your fear. Don't let it use you.

Lesson
We must stop holding ourselves back from opportunities to show and share our love.

Don't Deny Yourself

I had a friend in high school that only wanted to be referred to as 'so-and-so's girlfriend.' She made the guy the focal point of her life. She constantly wondered where he was going, what he was doing, and who he was going out and doing things with. She began to disregard her friendships and focused only on pleasing him.

I'll never forget the look in her eyes when she realized he didn't care about her as much as she cared about him. I will never forget the pain that took over her body as she cried violently when he chose to spend time with his friends rather than with her.

He was treating her disrespectfully in many ways. But in many ways he was simply rebelling because of her intense affection. The boy was trying to be a teenager and she was pretending to be an urban Juliet. Their romance was destined for failure.

We became friends through our boyfriends. Once we became close I finally had to ask her about the crazy relationship she was creating. Like so many women, she simply wanted to love and be loved. She wanted him to want her. She wanted him to love her deeply so that her world could feel full and complete. She was handing him her heart with hope that he could bring her happiness. Instead, he only brought her heartache because she was expecting so much of him.

In order to have happiness in a relationship you first have to be happy with yourself. You have to love your life. You have to do things that allow you to feel fulfilled. You increase your insecurities and anxiety when you are not happy with yourself and are dependent upon another person to fill the voids you feel in your life.

My friend found herself in such an unbalanced relationship because her and her boyfriend had different views and expectations of each other and the relationship. She thought she had found her future husband. He enjoyed being sexually active with her. She thought they would have the perfect life. He thought they were just having fun. Although this was a young couple, the patterns and potential problems are the same. We have to be clear about what we want from our relationships.

It is imperative that we discuss our expectations before committing to a relationship. In order to save your heart from some heartache, be specific about what you expect from your partner. Create a life that your partner can become a part of and enjoy with you. Do not be one of those women that revolve their whole life around a man. Maintain your lifestyle. Focus on what you love to do. Allow him to join you in activities you love. You'll find out that the right man will enjoy learning more about you and exploring life with you.

The best relationships allow the partners to become a part of one another's life. Trust me when I tell you that no man that loves you will ever want you to deny yourself, your happiness or the things you love, so that you may love him instead. A man wants to feel as though he's a major part of your life, not your only reason for existing. There is a big difference between a man choosing to make you happy and a man feeling obligated to make you happy.

Women who are so needy of love and affection can find themselves victims of mistreatment and bad relationships. If you have yet to find the love you want in your life, you must find it within yourself first. Focus on your needs. Create a life you love and cultivate your own happiness. Find a man that is happy with his life. Then you can start a relationship that consists of two people that love themselves, love their life, and perhaps find love with one another.

Lesson
The only person that can create happiness in your life is you.

Where Power Resides

You are more than your private parts. Unfortunately many women genuinely believe that the way to attract and keep a man is through sex. Attraction is very important and in many ways essential to a relationship.

If we are honest we will admit that we must be attracted to our life partner. The key words are that we must be attracted to them. We are not saying he has to be the "last man"—a term my sister friends and I use to describe an extremely handsome man. We are saying that when you look at that man, and into his eyes, you are attracted to him.

We are totally wrong when we believe that the thing that keeps a good man with us is our sexuality. The prize isn't where we think it is and several men have shared this with me. A few men told me that once a man matures and is ready for a loving, committed relationship, it is far more important that he have a woman that can be there for him, as the marriage vows say, for better or worse, for richer or poorer.

One of my best friends said he would choose a woman that would cook him dinner over one that would only offer him sex. He explained that because of the casual sex society we live in, sex could be had with any woman. But how many women would get up and make him a sandwich after a long day's work? I laughed, but he was serious and so were the other men I spoke with about relationships.

So if our power isn't in our private parts, then where is it? Our power is in our hearts, our spirits and our character. Yes, seriously. When a man is ready for a serious relationship he wants to know first and foremost that you are a good person and a good friend. He wants to know that you are financially independent and emotionally independent of your girlfriends.

Mature men do not want your every decision to be dependent upon what your girlfriends think and he most certainly does not want your girlfriends to know every detail of your relationship.

The men went on to tell me that they wanted women that allowed them to be the best man to the woman, without being judged by the woman's previous relationships or relationship experiences of her girlfriends or mother. Literally all the men said they would choose a woman with great character who knows her worth, has high self-esteem, and consideration for others and her man, over a woman that simply solves everything by offering up her sexuality.

I hate to make it sound as if all the decision-making is in the man's hands. In this instance I'm just giving you their viewpoint and letting you know that in the end, just as you want a man that is a good person and a good lover, a man wants the same thing. And as you know, in order to get what you want in a relationship you must reciprocate with the same type of love, appreciation, affection and attention.

Sometimes we treat our sister friends as essential parts of our lives and our men as disposable beings. Women and men appreciate a good friend and you should treat both with as much love and regard as you would want given to you.

Lesson
The characteristic that makes you attractive is the loving spirit you have and the way you share and show that love with others.

Hey Boo Boo

Almost every woman can share a time in her life when she had a Boo Boo the Fool moment. A Boo Boo the Fool moment occurs when a man you are involved with tells you something that is so outlandish that he is clearly either outright lying, thinks you're a fool or believes you're so deeply in love with him that you will disregard his very apparent fabrication. I haven't met a woman yet who hasn't had one of these moments or at least had a sister friend who had such a moment.

The funny and ironic thing about Boo Boo the Fool moments is that you are quite aware that the man thinks you would believe anything that comes out of his mouth. And sometimes we are to blame because we know we should call the man on his foolish behavior. Sometimes we allow him to finish his story so that we can look him in the eye and ask him without hesitation, do I look like Boo Boo the Fool? The most devastating moment though is when we know that the man is lying and we choose to accept his words and behavior anyway.

Sisters, the only way we can have better relationships in our lives is if we are honest with ourselves, and require that our friends and men are just as honest with us. The Boo Boo the Fool moments begin and end with us. During this moment we can either choose to play the role of the fool or we can listen to our intuition.

Your intuition will always give you the right answers for your life situations; you just have to be willing to listen. When a man is telling you something and the thought that he thinks you're stupid enters your mind then you are absolutely right. In that moment he thinks you are stupid enough to believe what he's saying. When a man tells you he was somewhere and your intuition tells you he was nowhere near where he's saying he was, you are right.

Now there is a tremendous difference between what your insecurities tell you, and what your intuition shares with you, and you must learn to know the difference.

If you are insecure you will believe that every man is lying and cheating on you. When you are insecure it is easy to believe that no one is worthy of your trust and that you are not worthy of being loved. When you are insecure you will settle for less than the best because you believe that the inferior treatment you are getting in your relationship is the best you can get. When you are insecure you will never believe a man when he tells you something in sincerity because your insecurity will make you believe that he will mislead, use, or hurt you in some-way, so you question his every move and word.

Your intuition, however, can decipher the truth from a lie, negative intentions from loving motivations, and a worthy man from one who doesn't deserve to be in your life at all.

Make sure to listen clearly so that you can tell whether it is your insecurity or your intuition responding to a situation, and listen to your intuition. Listening to your intuition will help you bring a stop to the Boo Boo the Fool moments, and help you have relationships in which your intelligence, heart and standards are respected, appreciated and honored.

Lesson
Respect and love yourself and then you will show others how to love and respect you.

Someone Else's Man

I have listened as men either denied being married, explained that they had an open relationship with their wife, or emphatically stated that things just "weren't right at home." Of course none of that nonsense ever worked on me. But eventually, if you have a strong opinion about something, a situation will occur to make you decide whether you really believe in your values and will continue to maintain them, or whether you will give in to temptation and change your mind.

I finally lived the experience of being alone in a city, not having many friends, and wanting a man to go to the movies or just have dinner with. I felt what it was like to want a hug, to hold hands or to be kissed. I understood what it felt like to want some companionship.

During one of those moments one of my sister friends confided that she had met a wonderful, sweet man that felt like a soul mate. She had been lonely for so long and now here he was to go to dinner, to the mall, to the park and to be intimate with. She stopped gushing about him just long enough to tell me not to judge the rest of what she had to say.

I took a deep breath and said, "Alright. Tell it."

She said, "He lives in another state."

"So what", I replied. "You sound so happy. You can make it work," I added, thinking she just needed to know that long-distance relationships could survive.

She paused again and said, "He's married."

The phone became quiet. All you could hear was my breath then her breath. We didn't speak for seconds. I felt all sorts of emotions go through my body. One stood out more than any other. I was angry.

Unfortunately, as every human does, I did judge her. I felt strongly that she was settling and justifying negative behavior. I understood completely that she had been feeling lonely and hadn't had a good relationship in a few years. But she was not looking at the complete picture and that was the fact that her happiness could be leading to someone else's misery. And whichever way you try to justify it, if one person is married then someone is getting hurt.

Like my friend, there are many women that date married men and every woman has her own reason for doing it. One woman may have known and dated the man prior to him getting married and simply does not respect or acknowledge the fact that he is now married. A woman may have met a man that clearly appears to be unhappy and she wants someone to spend time with.

There are women that say they are too busy to commit to a relationship and dating a married man just fits their guidelines—he stays awhile and then has to go home. There are a few women that are deceived and fall in love without knowing that their 'man' is married and then are too blinded by love to leave when they discover the truth.

Then there are the wives that are trusting their husbands and believe him when he says he's working late, is out with the boys, or has to go out of town on business. There are also wives that know their man is cheating and justify it by saying that "men will be men." Or they tolerate his behavior as long as he doesn't bring any evidence of it into their home.

We all know about the circumstances that allow married people to cheat. But do we ever ask the real reason? Do we care enough about humanity to make the married person be accountable for their relationship and tell them to go home and tell their wife or husband why they're unhappy or unfulfilled? No, we do not.

I know one thing for sure. If we're ever going to make life more fulfilling then we have to be aware of how we as individuals affect the world collectively. And any woman that tolerates, justifies, or participates in the demise of a marriage is affecting society as a whole. You're helping someone to be deceitful, allowing the man to deny his truth and avoid the reality of his relationship within the marriage. If the man has children with his wife, you're helping to affect that child's life and view about relationships.

It's all much deeper than having a moment with some man. It's much deeper than having someone to hold your hand and do things with. It is imperative that we, as women, understand that we never have to settle.

We deserve more than snippets of some man's time. We deserve more than to be someone's mistress. We deserve honest, loving relationships and the only way to get that is to give that. Respect relationships and open your life up to getting a respectful relationship. Honor marriage and open your life up to having a spouse that honors you.

Appreciate your time as a single person and stop thinking you're missing out on something or that some man has to make you whole. You are already whole and fulfilled and you were not put on this earth to settle for anything or anybody.

I understand what women are going through when they decide to date a married man. But no justification will ever make it right to do so. If a man is married and unhappy then he needs to let his wife know that before he brings his drama and blues to you. If a married man needs more out of a relationship then he needs to share that information with his wife, not you.

Women have to stop being deceived by these conversations married men have with them. I'm amazed at the number of women that feel special because a married man has shared with her how unhappy he is. Girl, please. You're not viewed as special. You're viewed as a hook-up; someone he can get his groove on with without needing to explain where he's been or what he's been doing before coming to your home. Come on, now! It's time we take responsibility for the relationships we enter into and the men we bring into our lives.

Lesson
We must set standards for our relationships and then we must have the strength to live up to them.

Love Pain

teardrops falling
feelings of rejection
insecurity burning
self-esteem shattering
pain in my heart
love pain
the end has come
no more letters
and visits
special times
and caresses
no more
he and I
anguish despair
anxiety anger
pain
love pain
tears of sweat
as I run from you
Mind-boggling activities

as I take myself away
from you
not friends
not enemies
has beens
was
were
no more are
or going to be
no more nothing

you there
I here
why are we gone
from one another
were we ever really together
my mind says no
my heart says pain
so we must have been

Cheaters Can Set You Free

It was 12 o'clock in the afternoon. The young woman in the bed was still resting. Well, she hadn't really rested since he left last night. He had kissed her on the cheek and said, "I'll be back." Now as the sun glared through the windows the young woman had to acknowledge one thing. The man she had been dating for two years had not come home last night.

It wasn't because he was in an accident. She was certain because she had called every hospital in the metro area. No, he had decided to stay out all night. He probably knew the minute he began to get dressed, as he took a long hot shower and put on his favorite cologne. He was probably planning his rendezvous when he avoided her eyes and went outside to make a phone call. So why was she just acknowledging the fact that her relationship had crumbled?

Suddenly there were footsteps on the front porch. She sat up and gazed out the window. It was him. He walked up the stairs as though he hadn't broken anyone's heart last night. As though he hadn't lied to a woman that had loved him dearly. Now what would she do? Why had he done this to her?

He simply walked in the house, said "Hey," and then went in the bathroom.

He never gave her a chance to scream. There were no moments to ask questions. Not only had he caused her immense pain, he also didn't seem to care about her reactions or emotions. She looked at the closed bathroom door then back at the glaring sunlight. Life wasn't supposed to be like this, she thought.

Being cheated on by someone you believe that you love is a devastating experience. The pain is almost indescribable. Any woman who has had her heart broken can instantly tap into the moment. The moment where the pain is so intense that you don't know whether to cry, scream, shout or just be still. You don't know whether your heart will ever be open to love again or whether you will ever trust another man. The intensity gives way to anger and disappointment. Then the moment of power begins.

Not every woman takes advantage of the moment of power. During the moment of power you have a chance to evaluate your relationship based on the facts only. You can push aside your emotional attachment to this man. You can push aside the many years or months you have spent loving him, laughing with him and being with him. You can push aside all the loving thoughts you may have had about this relationship. Then you take a deep breath and look at the relationship's history.

What led to the demise of the relationship? Did you both want the same things from the relationship? Did you discuss what was expected of one another? What did his actions and words say about how he felt about you?

Every man tells you how he feels about you. The way he tells you may vary. After our first date I began spending every weekend with this guy. He would always ask me what I wanted to do during the upcoming weekend. Then we would make our plans. On Sunday evening, just as I was about to head home, he would say, "You know I'm not ready for a relationship."

Now I can see that he was emotionally deceptive and sending me mixed signals. But at the time I liked him so much that I didn't actually hear him when he said he wasn't ready for a relationship. Instead, I chose to focus on the fact that we were spending every weekend together. I justified his inability to commit as fear. I told myself that his last relationship had ended badly and he was just a little hesitant. I mistakenly believed the relationship would eventually change and he would finally be ready.

After a few months he told me that he loved me and that he thought I was his soul mate. I smiled at my girlfriends with victory in my eyes but a lingering uneasiness in my heart. Although he was saying the things I wanted to hear I knew something was still not right. He flip-flopped back and forth from being ready for a relationship, wanting to marry me and enjoying our relationship to not being ready and not trusting women several times. So it shouldn't have come as a surprise when he didn't come home that night. I shouldn't have been totally shocked he could be so insensitive and intentionally hurtful.

I claimed my moment of power when I remembered those loving weekends and the inevitable Sunday night conversations. In that moment, I knew he had gotten used to me loving him but had never opened up his heart to loving me.

As women we have to listen to everything a man says. If you tell a man that you love him and he only replies that you are very special, you need to acknowledge that he does not love you. If you're falling in love with a man and all he says during conversation is that he'd like to be in love one day, then he is not falling for you. If you date a man for weeks or months and he always says he's not ready for a relationship, then he likes spending time with you but nothing more.

So how do we stop having relationships with cheating men? There's no perfect answer for that, but there are some practices we can implement to help us have better relationships. We need to stop having selective hearing. We must stop choosing to hear only what we want to hear. We must be clear about what we want, need and expect from a relationship in the very beginning and we have to be very honest with ourselves, and our potential partner, about those things. We should learn how to separate the emotions from the facts, and difficult as it may be, make our decision based on the facts.

The simple truth is if a man wants you, nothing can keep him away. If he doesn't want you, nothing can make him stay. After enduring my own moment of heartache I now know one thing for sure, we always know when someone is into us or not. You can deny that truth. You can make up excuses for his behavior. You can will yourself into believing that his feelings toward you will change. In the end the truth will prevail and you will see that your intuition was correct from the very beginning.

The greatest thing about a cheater is that his truth can set you free. You may have ignored your own intuition and pushed away your doubts. But when a man cheats on you, you have to confront your own truth. Will you continue to live a life in which you settle for less than the best and allow someone to give you less than you deserve? Or will you finally have the courage to choose better relationships, trust your intuition, and make sure all your needs are met?

Lesson
The actions of a man speak more clearly for him than his words ever will.

The Sister Who Cried Wolf

As soon as I began dating my boyfriend, one of my friends remarked that I was spending less time with her. Not wanting her to feel slighted I began making more of an effort to spend time with her. I called to see if she would like to do lunch or dinner or head out to a movie. No matter how often I called, I soon realized that I was constantly going to voice mail. Suddenly she was unreachable. Because I appreciated her friendship at the time, I continued to make additional efforts to reach out to her. I remained unsuccessful.

After a couple of weeks I received an extremely long email from her detailing how I had slighted her and hurt her feelings. Although I thought she was completely mistaken, I apologized.

There will be times in every relationship when we take responsibility for any wrongdoings whether intentional or not, just to save the relationship. But what do you do when a friend is constantly feeling slighted or hurt by you? Unless you have intentionally done something to hurt this friend their heightened sensitivity is going to wear on your last good nerve.

When I realized that this sister could turn her friendship off and on like a light switch and only remained happy with me as long as I did what she wanted or expected, her friendship began to mean less to me. It was almost like the friendship version of crying wolf.

We cannot allow anyone's insecurities to affect our energy. We cannot allow anyone's need for our time and energy to become overwhelming and stifling. There are some people that become envious of your joy and will find any possible reason to diminish it or put the attention back on them. You simply cannot stand for their drama or need for attention.

I know in my heart that I never intentionally hurt her feelings. Her level of importance in my life had not changed. Love does not constrict; it expands. Any woman that enters a loving relationship can still show love and friendship with her sister friend. Even though the amount of time spent together may change, the quality should never change.

Our friendship eventually ended because the sister had poor communication skills. It would take me weeks to decipher why she was upset or to receive a response to my phone calls. I have a lot of love for my friends, but I doubt I'll ever have enough patience to deal with someone that cannot explain their feelings and thoughts. And why should I, or you, have to bother with such drama? It's so unnecessary.

Friendship is a gift that should only be shared with people who are worthy of you.

Lesson
Open and honest communication is essential to all of our relationships in life. We have to be sure to see people the way they genuinely are rather than how we wish or believe them to be as individuals.

Move On Sister, Move On

I had an associate that I always looked at in wonder. She remained an associate and not a sister friend because I could not understand her choices. As I got to know her more I realized all we had in common was that we were both single mothers. Basically we had nothing to create or maintain a friendship. But she would call me every couple of months to update me on her life and try to find out what was going on in mine.

Every time she called I would try to give her the benefit of the doubt and hope and pray that something had changed in her life. Nothing in her world seemed to change though. As I look back on it now, I knew her for about three years. In those three years whenever we talked about her love life she always mentioned the same guys.

I mean she literally dated, and I use that word loosely, the same guys for three years. Not one of the guys ever showed any interest in committing to a relationship with her. Not one of the guys began their sexual relationship by being truthful with her.

So the question for me was, "How on earth does this sister tolerate, settle for and choose these type of relationships?"

Her situation led me to think about the choices I see so many women making. Professionally this associate of mine had everything she needed but it was what she wanted that was leading her to make insane choices in her relationships. It's the choice so many women make.

Many women I know have chosen mates that they are not equally yoked with simply because they do not want to be alone. They want someone to hug them, hold them or just be in the home with them.

This sister showed me that we have to be careful about what we put out into the universe. She wanted a man and some semblance of a family so badly that she tolerated unbelievable behavior from men that didn't want the same thing she wanted. I'm certain that she is still involved with these men because she is not expecting a great man to come into her life.

As you know, what you expect is what you get. So she continues to meet men who are unwilling or unable to commit and have limited time to spend with her.

These types of relationships will not end until the woman stops accepting demeaning relationships.

As women we have to make one another more accountable for the relationships we choose. I always asked this sister why she continued to see these men and she never responded by saying more than, I don't know. Every time she called me I told her that she deserved better and had to stop settling. Then her response would be, I know. But I never wavered on my point and that's what we have to do as women.

Tell the woman the truth the same way you would want someone to tell you. Don't sugarcoat it. When the guy does something to your girlfriend that should be unacceptable, you need to question her about it. Don't just tell her how bad he is mistreating her. Ask her why she's dealing with, tolerating and choosing to be in that type of relationship. Ask her why she puts up with it. Put her on the spot. I know so many times the guy has done some outlandish thing and as girlfriends we start talking about how bad the guy is but what about talking about how crazy your girlfriend is for putting up with the stuff? Let's start the dialogue there—by making each other expect more from relationships.

Believe me, I know it's much easier to think, "What the hell is wrong with this girl?" However, we are not being the best women and friends we can be if we do not share our honest opinion and ask our girlfriends why they are not demanding more from their relationship or moving on to something better.

It is imperative that women stop talking about one another and start talking to one another about our life choices. There is always a point in life where you or one of your girlfriends truly needs to move on from a bad situation and just needs honest advice or inspiration and motivation from someone in order to make their decision. Let's be a spark for change and help one another have better relationships.

Lesson
Friendships are a loving relationship, in which honest communication is essential. If you truly love and want the best for your friend then you must do your best to always guide them to the best choices for their lives. Remind your friend of how phenomenal she is and how much she deserves love. To love your friend is to give her the advice, encouragement and inspiration you would want given to you. This will help all women to have a better view of themselves and expect better treatment in their relationships.

Do You Need A Divorce?

The conversation began innocently enough. There was loud laughing and story telling. By the time the laughter had dwindled there were two clear messages that had been provided. You're an enabler and you need to divorce yourself from that person. Could it be true? Was I being an enabler?

I quickly scanned my memory and thought of my chaotic relationship with my daughters' father. I had clearly been an enabler in that relationship. Because I didn't want to believe that I had helped in creating such a hellish life, I led myself to believe that his problems were not that bad. I told myself he wasn't as bad as most. But eventually I had to see the light and make a choice to save myself.

So the words enabler and divorce resonated with my being. Yes, you are absolutely right, I agreed. I will make changes right away.

I know so many of us allow people to remain a part of our lives for various reasons. However if we are honest with ourselves we clearly know when it is time to separate. In fact, when we are honest we will know that it is time to divorce ourselves from this person.

Dictionary.com defines divorce as: To cut off; separate or disunite.

As we deal with life, many people will hide from the truth and choose to pretend that everything is fine. A few people will stop allowing anyone, including family members, to disrespect them in anyway. A few more will choose to stop accommodating those who never consider their feelings or their time. And instead a few of us will choose to create a new family structure, to form new friendships and to hold people and ourselves up to higher standards.

One thing I know for sure is that if you settle in one area of your life then by definition you are settling. Either you are settling or you are not. There is no in-between.

So I remind you to stop allowing yourself to be misused. Stop allowing people to take you for granted. Stop holding back your words when the truth begs to be let out. In order for us to truly live a life we love, we must be honest with ourselves and hold the people in our lives accountable for their actions.

Divorce yourself from the people who will hold you back from your greatness. Don't allow any person, whether mother, father, sister, brother, auntie, or uncle, get in the way of your blessings. You deserve the best and the only way to receive the best is to expect and accept only the best.

Lesson
There can be times when the opinions and actions of others are affecting your ability to have love in your life. Everyday you are either choosing to let them block you or you are choosing to release yourself from them so that you can move toward love.

Bring Me Greatness

Have you ever had to walk away from someone that you loved from your soul? You knew you had to walk away, because as good as they were and as much potential as they possessed, they were not good for you? Those are the hardest walks to make. Especially when God has told you to walk away. I have learned that God doesn't really like repeating himself so we have to listen that first time. But when you walk away from someone you love it can feel as though you're stepping in wet concrete.

The lesson we need to learn is that even if a man is a good person, it doesn't mean he is good for you. The most courageous thing you can do for your spirit is to walk through the pain. Just deal with the moment and realize that it will pass. You will get through it. You will get over it. You will get past it. The best gift you can give yourself is knowledge of when to let go and how to free yourself from drama. Choose love, not misery. Choose peace, not drama. Choose who you want in your life, don't always let people choose you.

A good friend of mine always prayed for a relationship. Eventually she entered into a relationship with a man that seemed good in the beginning. He was loving, affectionate, attentive and dependable. They became inseparable and he moved into her home. Then, of course, the truth emerged. Although he was loving and sweet he was also unbelievably broke. In basic terms they met each other's needs in one way—he needed a place to live and she needed a man to love. It was a perfect match in relationship hell.

It took her awhile to realize the magnitude of the relationship she entered because she was focused on the sweet things they did together. Who wouldn't be sweet if they didn't have to pay rent, pitch in on groceries, or help with a light bill? But, I digress. In all honesty, he was one of the sweetest men she had ever dated. He was a good man. He just wasn't good for her.

So many women have found themselves in unbalanced relationships at some point in their lives. We simply have to get to a point where we stop loving for potential and love for right now. Do you love the man for who he is or for the man you think he can become? Is the man you love everything you would ever hope for or is he lacking in some areas? Are you putting up with something you normally wouldn't because you don't want to be alone?

The truth of the matter is we stay in deteriorating and unfulfilling relationships for a few reasons. Usually we stay because we don't want to enter the dating world again, we're afraid of being alone, we've allowed a man to have more worth in our lives than he really deserves, or we're making excuses for the man in some way.

A woman always knows when she has a great thing. She also knows when she has something she should get rid of. We just need to be honest with ourselves. Either we're going to wait until greatness enters our lives or we're going to deal with and tolerate mediocre, good but not great, kind of fulfilling relationships.

During my life I've learned that God may give you good in order to see if you're ready for the great things He has in store for you. He may give you something good to see if you'll appreciate it and then move on to the phenomenal thing that's coming up. So now when something's good I pray to God, if this is for me then let it be but if you have something better for me then make me ready for it.

Bring me greatness every time. I pray for that.

Lesson
We have to be willing to let go of the mediocre things in our life and go toward the greatness God has waiting for us.

Step Three—Expect What You Want

o o o o o o o o o o o o o o o o o o o o o o o o o o o o o o o o o o o o o o o

A simple truth I have learned is that love expects love. In order to have all the love you deserve, you must expect love to manifest in your life. Your heart and your mind must want to experience and believe in the power of love. If your heart longs for love but your mind tells you that you are not worthy, or that every man will break your heart, you will sabotage yourself. If you truly want a loving relationship your heart and your mind must be in sync.

Promise Yourself

To be so strong that nothing can disturb your peace of mind.
To think only of the best, to work only for the best and to expect only the best.
To be too large for worry, too noble for anger, too strong for fear, and too happy
to permit the presence of trouble.

Christian Dwight Larson

Good Woman?

The book signing had just ended and only one woman remained. She came toward me with her book and then gently sat down next to me. As she handed me the book her eyes caught mine and she said, "I have a problem that I need some help with."

I asked her what was wrong and she took a breath.

"I feel like I'm having a hard time finding love and a good relationship," she said. "I don't know if it's just not the right timing. Maybe God doesn't think I'm ready, but I would love to have a good relationship with a good man," she said quickly.

I asked her about the type of men she was attracting and what she considered a good relationship. She believed that God was an essential element of every relationship and that people must be equally yoked. Then her truth was revealed; she was dating married men. She tried to justify it by saying that the men weren't married when she met them. She explained that the men had gotten married after dating her and were now in unhappy marriages.

So I asked her, "How can you keep asking God to bless you with a good relationship and a good man when you're not being a good woman?"

Well girlfriend looked as though I had slapped her or perhaps she wanted to slap me. Either way, she sat back stiffly on the chair and looked at me.

Her words and demeanor quickly became defensive and she said, "Well I'm not the one that is married. They chose to marry those women. They are the ones cheating on and lying to their wives. They are pursuing me."

I looked at her, smiled and said, "You are helping them to lie to and cheat on their wives. You're helping them to dishonor their relationships and commitment. You are showing them that if they are unhappy in their marriage they can seek comfort with another woman rather than discuss the problems with their wives. You are enabling this whole thing."

Then I asked again, "How are you being a good woman?"

So many times in life we try to shift the blame to other people. Only a few people ever take full responsibility for their actions. I believe as women that want powerful, God-filled, loving relationships we have to be honest about our actions and take responsibility for our choices. Every relationship you enter into should be filled with love. Every relationship you enter into defines who you are and makes a statement about you to the world.

Have you ever noticed a couple and all you could do was smile because you could feel the love in the air around them? Then what type of energy do you imagine a woman having an affair with a married man would generate? And what type of man would a woman that condones infidelity attract?

If you want love then you must be a loving person. If you want a good man you must be a good woman. Believe good men exist and stop tolerating mediocre relationships. If you want the best life and relationship God can offer you then you must only expect and accept the best. God can only give you what you are ready for and if you choose to be a part of dishonest relationships then you cannot receive your full blessings.

In order to have the loving relationship that you want, you must honor the relationships of others. How and why would God bless you with a good man when you cannot respect the commitment a man and a woman have made to one another?

After listening to me intently as I talked about loving relationships, she sat forward and said, "Those are their relationships. They're not honoring their relationships. I'm not in a relationship with them. How can what they're doing affect me?"

This time I was the one with a look of disbelief on my face.

She sat there, waiting for an answer. So I explained to her that I truly believe in karma. You know the saying, what goes around comes around? Whatever you do in life will come back to you in some way.

It may not be as simple as you cheated with a married man so your future husband will cheat on you. It could be that you're tolerating mediocrity in your life in someway and you cannot seem to understand your life purpose, or you feel a void in your life, or your finances are in disarray, or your sister friends don't seem as supportive as you'd like, or you feel like people aren't giving you their best or being the best friend possible, or you're job is unfulfilling, you can't find the right church, your weight is fluctuating and you feel like you can't control it. Your life choices can show up in many ways in your life so it is essential that we do our part to attract and receive the best life has to offer.

Before I left the signing I had to let this woman know, If you sleep with a married man you are basically saying that you don't respect relationships of any kind and that will affect all of your friendships and relationships.

If you tolerate a married man cheating on his wife then you are excusing his behavior and you will live your life based on excuses. If you listen as a man rants about his wife but never advise him to talk to her and try to work it out with her then your lines of communication with your friends and loved ones will not be at their best.

Every choice you make affects your life. So if you are destined for greatness and want good in your life then you must be good—be a good woman, be a good friend, be a good lover. And expect and demand that everyone in your life be good to themselves and those they claim to love.

Lesson
If you want the best life and relationship God can offer you then you must only expect and accept the best.

Be Yourself

"I don't want him to see me smoking," she said, and thrust the cigarette into my hand.

My question was, "Why are you hiding who you are?"

So many times women and men create a false persona for one another, especially in the beginning of a relationship. I wonder how much easier relationships and our lives would be if we simply chose to be ourselves fully and honestly everyday.

When the reality of being a single mother hit me, I felt somewhat angry, frustrated, and afraid of my choices in men. I gave away my power to choose and instead allowed the men to choose me to be in their life. My standards lowered as I tried to fit into the man's world. I thought single motherhood had eliminated my chances of having a happy, loving relationship with a man so I settled for what was available. The key words in this brief story tell the story of many women. Words such as: afraid, gave away, allowed to be chosen, lowered standards, tried to fit, and settled.

We have to get to a point where we love who we are today without shame, embarrassment, guilt or complexes. Our choices of yesterday do not have to dictate where we go in the future. We must realize that we have the power to make choices every day. And within those choices, is the chance to choose whom we bring into our life. It is the power of knowing that we are worthy of and deserve love and happiness. We must never forfeit who we are at our core in order to make someone else feel happy and fulfilled.

Life is not about changing who you are in order to have love. Life is about being exactly who your spirit says you should be and attracting love to you.

Stop changing for men. Stop changing for your family and friends. Stop being less than the beautiful person that you are. At your core you are love, beauty, strength, courage, hope, and faith. Believe those things and they will come to you. Deny yourself these things and you will always find ways to settle in your life, justify unacceptable behaviors, and evade true happiness and peace.

Live your life based on your truth. Set standards for yourself and know the difference between sacrifice and compromise.

Lesson
In order to experience true love you must begin with loving yourself unconditionally.

Take Your Time

There are too many people in the world that can say, "I didn't know him or her as well as I thought I did."

The reality is that you probably did know whether something was off about the person, you just chose not to accept it or believe it.

I had been dating a guy for about two weeks when suddenly I just looked up at him and wondered why we were spending so much time together and I instantly knew that he was not the love of my life. But he was a kind and considerate guy. So even when he noticed something was wrong and questioned me about it, I dismissed my thoughts and said nothing was wrong.

Eventually the relationship ended because my feelings of unhappiness continued to grow and finally I became so miserable in the relationship, despite his kind ways, that I had to end the relationship.

When I looked back on the situation I would always wonder how much time and months I wasted because I didn't trust my intuition. I learned to listen to that small voice that tells me what is right or wrong for me because our intuition is how God speaks to us and our intuition can guide us to making better choices in our lives.

There is nothing that can be hidden from the spirit. Though people try to avoid the truth, the truth cannot be hidden. Though people try everyday to justify their behavior and the behaviors of others, the truth cannot be hidden. If we take the time to listen to our spirit we can make better choices. And in relationships, if we would just take the time to get to know one another, and trust our intuition, we could save ourselves from dealing with a lot of drama and heartache.

Give yourself the power of hindsight in the here and now. Slow down and get to know people. There is no reason to rush and bring someone into your world. Let things develop. Give yourself a chance to know a person in their good and bad moments. Give yourself a chance to know whether someone is a true friend or not.

We have to stop creating lives of stress and frustration. You have the power to end the cycles you're living in. But you have to learn how to take your time.

Lesson
Give people an opportunity to earn your friendship and love.

Expectations

I firmly believe that we do not set out to love our lives because no one has shown us how to live lives we love. Many of us also do not have loving relationships because we have not seen a loving relationship in action. Regardless of our family structure, so many of us state that we saw negativity in our parents.

Unfortunately we expected our parents to be perfect beings and mold us into loving, responsible beings. In a perfect world it would work out like that for all of us. But the reality is that many of us have not seen ideal relationships and this affects our life in many ways. Fortunately, our lives do not have to be limited to what we have seen. Rather, we can choose to create a new paradigm for our personal relationships.

Although you may have never seen a man treat a woman with kindness and a look of love in his eyes, you do realize that type of affection exists? Although you may have seen your mother treat you as the most precious thing in the world and treat her husband with disregard, you do realize that love expands and you can love your children and your husband fully?

Although you may have seen your parents in an abusive relationship, you do know that no man should ever hit you? Although you may have seen your parents live life in financial disarray, you do know that you can be taught to manage your finances well?

I assure you, without a shadow of a doubt, that you can create the opposite of what you have seen in life. I advise you to stop living your life based on the experiences of your parents. They chose their life experiences and now you need to choose yours. How do I know you can create these loving, wonderful relationships although you've never seen one in action? Because, we are all capable of creating what we need to have a fulfilling life.

Inventors do it every day. An inventor created the wheel, the automobile, the stoplight, and many things that we now call necessities. But prior to them creating these wonderful devices, these things did not exist and were not conceived of until the investor thought, What if?

So I advise you to change your outlook on love and your life. Ask yourself, What if? What if I chose to love my life? How would that affect every decision I make? What if I chose to genuinely love this man even though my heart was broken in the past and every sister I know is in a bad relationship? What if my experiences are different? What if the love I have within and the trust I have in God can get me through every lesson and situation that comes my way? What if I am meant to be loved, to love, be wealthy and have a peaceful, joyful home? What if I could create my ideal world? What if I learned from the mistakes and the positive experiences of my parents and used those lessons to create better relationships and a better life for myself?

Something I know for sure is that God can make the impossible possible. So believe and trust in the possibilities and teach yourself how to create a great life.

Lesson
Your expectations can limit or free you in life and love.

Open My Heart

In life there are lessons
the heart must learn
a gentle reminder
that we are spirit
here for growth
a time for inspection
to realize our worth
to feel how beautiful it is
to be loved
and cherished
and adored
      My love
my heart
it is so hard
to realize there are lessons
which my soul requests
but my mind can't understand
so difficult to understand the why
of spiritual growth
there are lessons in life

this is true
so I'll open my heart to you
in expectation
of my soul expanding
my heart loving
my soul reaching
a new level
of its essential evolution

Faith Is Not Selective

I have a few sister friends that fully believe and acknowledge that God has worked wonders in their life. They know that whatever difficulty they are dealing with can be resolved with prayer and reliance on God. In a moment of pain or insecurity they know how to hand their problem over to God. They trust that the power of God will work in their lives. Yet, with woman after woman there is one situation in which their faith becomes a little shaky, doubt enters their mind, and they just don't know if it will work out the way they want it to. The one situation they all have doubts about deals with relationships.

I've seen a woman that was on death's door put all her faith in God to get her through that painful time. She survived and came back to health with a renewed spirit. But when asked how she felt about relationships, she admitted that she had practically given up on having a good relationship. She had become disappointed by her former relationships.

So many women block their blessings by becoming jaded. The way I view everything is based on one philosophy—God brought this person or this situation into my life therefore it is meant to test me, bless me or teach me. All of my sister friends know one of my favorite quotes is from the movie *Amistad.* Long story short, there was no word for "try" in the African language of the captives. In their language, you either do something or you do not. There is no in between.

For those women that have strong faith in every other area of their life I have one question, How can we possibly trust God to bless us fully in our finances and in our health but not in our relationships? You trust that God is going to work things out in your life right? Then you have to trust him fully in ALL things. There is no hesitation or doubt or let me wait and see. You trust God and the experience. Expect the best and you will receive the best. No you may not receive the best from that specific man. But because your intention is to receive the best, that man will be removed from your life so that the best can enter your life.

There is no reason to be emotionally stressed or anxious about anything. Whenever you do those things you are not allowing your spirit to trust in God. You cannot have wavering faith. You must have faith and belief that God controls your life. God already has everything planned for you. Trust in that. God knows your needs. God knows your heart. We don't have to worry about anything because God will provide whatever we need. It may not be what we want but we'll get what we need.

One of my favorite proverbs says, "He who deliberates fully before taking a step will always remain on one leg." Meaning you can't walk fully into God's blessing if you're sitting there doubting or wondering whether this is right for you. If you assert yourself as a child of God then the only thing that can enter your life, your space and use your energy are things of God. You don't even have to worry about anything else because your faith and trust will allow God to remove the negative for you.

Have you ever watched beads of water hit a windshield? Although the rain may be coming down hard, you know that you will not get wet. That's how the negative stuff can be removed from your life. Negative thoughts may come into your mind but they will never affect you if you trust God fully with everything.

I firmly believe that we will get what we set our minds upon obtaining. So if we want loving relationships then we must believe in that possibility. We must see that loving relationship as though it already exists. We must know that the same God we have immense faith in to heal us, to help us and to love us, knows the needs of our hearts and will meet our needs when the time is right. But don't ever give up on love; you need love in order to feel the beauty of life. Love is essential to our growth and necessary for our spirit.

Do not have selective faith. Don't just believe that God will answer your prayers about your health and finances. God hears all your prayers. Remember though, that we can only receive what we already believe we deserve and are going to get. How many times have you heard a story of someone explaining with joy that they knew God would bring them through? Did you ever ask yourself why or how they got through? More than likely, it's because they didn't look at their previous health scares nor did they look at statistics. They simply had faith that they would be blessed. If we have faith and know that God will bless us in those ways then we must trust that he will bless us with love in our lives as well.

Lesson
Faith is not selective. If you believe in the power of God then you trust that God can work in your life in all ways.

Love Doesn't Stop You

One of my favorite people in history is Harriet Tubman. Harriet put her life on the line to help hundreds of slaves escape to freedom. She came back to get her husband only to find that he had married someone else and refused to follow her into the free Northern states. Based on the history at the time, their union could have been arranged by her owner (Her husband, John Tubman was a free man when they married) and so maybe there was no deep love between Harriet Tubman and her husband. But for a spiritual perspective we are going to assume that a woman that loved freedom so much and lived so courageously also must have loved deeply.

So when Harriet returned to find her husband shacked up with someone else, who knows what she felt in her heart at that moment? I know she must have felt some pain. She must've experienced some heartache. She may have shed a few soul tears. She may have truly broken down and cried. But then she got up. She kept walking. She kept moving. And she left that man right there and went about her spiritual purpose of helping others find freedom.

She never allowed the love she had for this man to stop her from living her purpose. She never let the bond she had with him stop her from doing what she was meant to do. Harriet knew that there are choices we have to make in life. The first priority must be our happiness. Harriet knew that she could not change a person's mind or status in life. But if they want to change, then we can definitely help. She knew the difference between helping someone and becoming stagnant with someone. And once she made a commitment to you, to help you, she was going to give you her focus, energy and strength.

We need to make the same type of commitment in our lives, with our purpose being spiritual fulfillment, mental freedom, emotional peace and experiencing glorious love. We must stop making excuses for people and for ourselves. We must stop being stagnant and start living life. Yes, we may have many obstacles before we get to our spiritual and financial freedom. But we've got to get up, keep walking, and keep moving.

A better life is out there if you stop holding yourself back and stop letting other people hold you back. We have got to start thinking from our spiritual best interest rather than our emotional interests. If Harriet had stopped for love's sake, or out of fear, she would have remained a slave. She didn't stop loving, she just knew when to let go and find her freedom. We have to do the same thing.

Lesson
Sometimes you have to walk away from someone you love in order to have the freedom and happiness you deserve.

The Queen Is Here

When my friend and I were teenagers we would make every guy we dated refer to us as queens. Literally when they began to say our name we would stop them and say, 'No, I'm a queen and you should call me that.' God knows they probably wanted to call us something else. But every time we suggested the name change the guy would acquiesce and call us queen. We had been reading about African history and the royalty from certain African countries, the respect the women commanded, and how they remained beautiful while doing their part to rule the land. And we wanted to be the same thing—powerful women who ruled the world.

We may have been overbearing in our desire to be referred to only as queens. However, we did something at a very young age that has lasted throughout our dating years. As I've gotten older I realize how significant our royalty phase was to our development as women. We demanded respect from every man that chose to be involved with us. We never allowed ourselves to be disrespected, mistreated or abused. We haven't always had perfect relationships but we've had the perfect foundation for years.

You teach people how to treat you. You teach them how to love you and how to pamper you. You show the men in your life what they need to do to get a smile from you or to get into your heart. You teach a man whether to treat you as though you are royalty or not.

As I get older, all of my best friends have jokingly said at one point or another, Well yes, Princess Natasha or Look here, Queen Tasha. So although I'm not verbally saying, 'Call me Queen Natasha,' my essence says it nonverbally—I am a queen and I deserve to be treated well.

So, how do you deserve to be treated? Please don't tell me you don't feel worthy of love or that you don't feel like a queen. Can you pretend for a moment and just allow yourself to slip into the mode of royalty? Imagine what it feels like to be treated as though you were precious. Imagine what it is like for a man to look into your eyes and wait anxiously for your next word. Imagine your boyfriend or husband saying, Baby, what can I get for you? Imagine your friends saying, Girl I thought about you and did this for you. Are you imagining? Can you feel the greatness rising up inside of you almost making you want to scream at the world, "I Am A Queen!"

You are a queen. You deserve the best. You deserve the best from your friends, your family, your man and everyone else in your life. And as a true queen you must treat those around you as though they deserve the best as well. Enjoy your throne.

Lesson
A person will only treat you the way you allow her or him to treat you.

A Touch of Kindness

Have you ever had someone test your kindness? You know, you do so much for them and they keep taking and taking? They give you some half-hearted thank-you and then show up again when they need something from you. You know the type of people that have you wondering whether being nice is the smart thing to do?

There are some people that do not understand the power of kindness. They do not understand that kindness is an action. Kindness always works best when it is given and received.

There are some people in your life that will keep taking from you until you finally tell them they have crossed the line. People always laugh at me when I say, I'm kind but no one has ever told me I'm too nice. They think I'm joking. I'm not.

There comes a time when some people will become like leeches on your spirit and you will not survive in a healthy manner if you don't cut them loose. We have got to stop trying to do everything for everybody. You have to know when you are giving too much. You always know when someone is using you and in order for it to change or stop, you are going to have to call the person on her or his behavior.

There's nothing wrong with being kind. What's wrong is not receiving appreciation for your kindness. In order to stop a person's habit of misusing your kindness, you're going to have to change your behavior. And that does not mean that you stop being a kind person. It means you let people know that you need and deserve a thank you. You deserve to be appreciated for all that you do and you should appreciate what others do for you.

Lesson
All of your relationships, friend and intimate, should be balanced. The people in your life should appreciate and never take your kindness for granted.

80

All Or Nothing

A sad reality is that most people prefer to talk about change rather than commit to making change. So many people say "If I just had the opportunity … If I just had the time … If someone would just give me a chance." They wind up on their deathbeds with regrets because they never got out of the "If" zone and into the realm of creating real changes. They live and die based on, "If I."

Jesus said there would be poor always. Poor can be subjective though. It can mean poor in spirit, poor in finances, poor in courage or poor in strength.

In everything that I do, I always try to stick to my goal of empowering the community one spirit at a time. I believe that together we can change this world. If we truly focus on becoming the best we can be we will affect the lives of others in an amazing way. So our collective goal must be to be rich—rich in spirit, rich in finances, rich in courage, rich in strength and rich in wisdom.

Throughout the history of the world there have been people that fought for freedom and those that decided that fighting was too difficult. There are people that are complacent and stagnant in their lives and people that fight everyday to learn more about themselves and the world. There are those that hope for change and those that make change. There are those who create their destiny and those that allow their lives to be created for them. Which side are you on?

Are you a fighter or a dreamer?

Are you a talker or a do-er?

Are you going to be rich or poor?

When you do not reach out and do everything you can to achieve your dreams you limit your life.

Have you ever witnessed or seen a movie in which a woman is being battered by her husband? The police come to the scene and try to pull the man off of the woman. And then what does the woman do? That's right, she starts screaming at and fighting the police. She gets upset with them for trying to save her. Then she starts defending the man that was just beating her down. Why? Because she's too afraid to change her life. She's giving her power away out of fear. She's willing to stay in hell because she's not sure what type of life she could create on her own.

Now we may not be in this exact situation. But if we're not living our dream life then we need to stop defending the life we are living. Stop stifling yourself. Stop holding yourself back. Stop making excuses and start living a life in which you are in control.

In order to find love in your life you first have to love your life. Just getting by in life is not enough. Having just enough is not enough. Living a life of mediocrity is a self-imposed hell that can be changed.

Lesson
You choose who you are. You determine the live you will live, the people you will love, and to what and whom you will share your time and energy with.

Step Four—Let Your Intuition Guide You

○ ○

We have been given a great gift. The gift of intuition. Our intuition speaks clearly to us and tells us whether a person is right for our life or not. If you truly want better relationships and more loving experiences than you must let your intuition guide you. Your intuition will tell you more than your eyes can see and more than your ears can hear. Your intuition will allow you to literally feel and sense whether a person deserves to be in your world. And if you are ready for better relationships then all you need to do is listen, pay complete attention to and make decisions based on your intuition.

The best love is the kind that awakens the soul and makes us reach for more, that plants a fire in our hearts and brings peace to our minds.

—*The Notebook*, 2004

Just An Illusion

I looked at the guy intently. He didn't know I was staring. I was in deep thought. My energy had completely changed when I looked directly at him. I looked at him and wondered how I had gotten into a relationship with him. I wondered exactly where this relationship was headed and why we were spending so much time together. Shouldn't I be happy about spending so much time together?

A few seconds before I had thought I was happy. I wondered what changed and then he caught me staring. He asked me what was wrong. There it was, my moment to tell the truth and say something about the changing feelings inside of me. Instead, I said nothing was wrong and looked away as though he were overreacting. Why didn't I tell the truth?

How do you tell someone who appears to be so happy being with you that you're not happy at all? How do you share that information when they haven't done anything to hurt or upset you? I am so happy that God has given me the wisdom to answer that properly. I know now that it is always wise and best to tell your truth. You see, I could have ended that relationship right then and there. But in denying my truth I allowed this relationship to go on for years.

I have endured and seen other women stay in relationships that are unfulfilling because they didn't have a 'concrete' reason for ending the relationship. The guy wasn't abusive or inattentive. In most cases the guys were decent but something was missing in the relationship. We have to think clearly from now on and know that we don't need a 'concrete' reason.

If your spirit is telling you that you are unhappy or unfulfilled then you need to make some life changes. We know that we cannot change another person so the only decision should be to change ourselves. How can we make our own lives better and more fulfilling?

That relationship taught me to never compromise my happiness. We deserve to be happy. We deserve to wake up with smiles on our faces, peace in our heart and God on our minds. We deserve to wake up glowing. We deserve to have a partner that we adore and couldn't imagine living without. We deserve to look at our partner with a huge smile as we think about how much we love him. And our partner deserves the same. We all deserve to have someone adore and love us completely and honestly.

So as spiritual beings we cannot keep one another or ourselves in unfulfilling relationships or situations. For years I knew that I didn't adore the man I was involved with. I had simply grown tired of dating and used to him. So while I was settling, he was being held back from having a relationship with a woman that adored him. In this situation, we have to understand that there can be better situations and relationships for you and him. There are no perfect women and men but there can be women and men that are perfect for one another.

We have to be willing to let go of the idea of settling. We have to stop enduring unfulfilling situations. We have to have the courage to leave situations in which we are unhappy. The only thing stopping you from telling your man that you want more from a relationship, just not from him, is you. The only thing that stops you from leaving a dead-end job and cultivating your talent, starting your dream business or finding another job is you. You have to be willing to make the changes. You have to stop letting fear and indecision block you from having a wonderful life.

I know what it is like to feel stuck in life. I know what it's like to tell yourself that you made a decision and now you have to deal with it. I know that at times we can block our own greatness because we do not acknowledge that just as we had a choice in the past, we now have a choice in our future.

So maybe you've stayed in a job or relationship a little longer than you anticipated. What are you going to do about that now? Are you going to think about what could have been done in your life or are you going to create a new life from this point? Until the moment we leave this earth we will always have the power to make new decisions. We will always have a truth inside of us that either sits inside us desperately waiting to get out and be lived, or we will live everyday of our lives with our truth being expressed in our lives. It is all a choice.

Although you may feel stuck in life, that type of thinking is really an illusion, because you are quite capable of making a different choice right now and getting 'unstuck.' Don't limit yourself. I know one thing for sure, you will always have a moment to get out. Just as I had that moment to end the relationship, you will have a moment where your intuition speaks so loudly that the words will spill from your mouth. You will clearly say, "I am not happy. I am not fulfilled. I want to end this relationship. I want to leave this job."

You will come to a point in your life where you will utter your truth. You simply have to be prepared for the moment and allow it to happen. If you do not tell the truth when your intuition clearly tells you to say something, you will only delay your happiness and fulfillment.

It is essential that we place our happiness as a priority in our lives. So many times we stay in relationships and jobs because of what others will think about it if we leave. Do you care more about what others think or about your happiness? The moment you know that your happiness matters more than the opinions of others, you will change your life.

When people meet me now they cannot believe that it took me so long to end a relationship or that I didn't speak up and say what I wanted. I don't come off as shy or inhibited. I usually say exactly what comes to my mind in a nice way. I've gotten to this point because I know how many years I sacrificed by being afraid to speak my truth. I know now that I will never deny my truth again and I hope you do the same.

Lesson

You are more powerful than you acknowledge, more talented than you give yourself credit for, more certain of what to do with your life than you think, capable of giving more love than you are right now, and fully prepared to live a better life than you are in this moment. You simply must decide to take a step toward living as a powerful, phenomenal person and stop making excuses for yourself.

The Fair

Around and Around and
Around and Around
making you dizzy
giving feelings of nausea
circles
head spinning
lies
jealousy
all a part of false love
they tell you they love you
then have their way with everything in sight
including you and your mind
this is not love
not even infatuation
it is settling
for what you should be rejecting
if you stop to give time to liars
they will pull you into their world
a fairy tale world
where all goes their way and they call you

Alice, Dorothy
or something other than your name
this is not love
do not be fooled
you are worth more than this
any person that brings you more heartache than joy
only adds to your stress
let him go
he is not yours
his only girl is his lies

get off that merry-go-round
hell get out of the carnival
find a man
let the boys finish growing
then you can walk with dignity and know
what you are in

Look At Me

Look At Me
not at my smile
not at my body
Look At Me
Look at my eyes
that is where my spirit lies
that is where
truth be told
my vulnerabilities unfold
Look at my eyes
I will not mislead you
nor do I want you to waste my time
my soul is precious
a gift from God
Look At Me
remember
I am rare
beautiful
intelligent
spiritual

loving
a woman with feelings
Look At Me
get to know me
my feelings are your feelings
for I see your side
I know where your spirit lies
did anyone ever tell you
you have beautiful eyes?

Eyes Of The Soul

I'm certain you've heard the saying, "The eyes are the window of the soul." But have you really looked at a man to see his soul shine through his eyes? As you grow in wisdom, you learn to tell the difference between the look of lust, infatuation or love exuding through a man's eyes. If we are honest with ourselves we will know in an instant what he wants from and sees in us. The question is, do we trust our judgment?

Many times women foolishly believe that a relationship can begin with lust and end with love. The significant difference is you must see the ability to love emanate through the man's eyes and shine upon you. You must see that he sees you as more than a sexual object and views you as a unique woman worthy of love and respect.

I look into the eyes of every person that speaks to me. I used to feel uncomfortable around people that couldn't make eye contact with me. You know the type of people that look at the wall or your forehead as they have a conversation with you? For some reason they cannot make or maintain contact so they just talk around you? I'm certain there are many reasons why people do not make eye contact. But you must have eye contact because the eyes will tell you the intentions of the spirit of that person.

The eyes will always tell you a person's depth and warmth. The eyes of a person will tell you whether a person can be friend or associate or if you need to move away from the person as quickly as possible.

We all have the ability to look into the eyes of a person and see their spirit, we simply have to trust and honor our first thought about the person. Their eyes, and yours, will never lie.

Lesson
The eyes of a person give us a glimpse into their soul.

Out of There

On a pedestal
looking down
at everyone
laughing at the boys and men
who were vying for
your position
smiling at me
looking so proud
and strong
inside a child
nothing but a boy
my God
I'm in love with a boy
even put him on my pedestal
I'm going to have to dethrone him
he's trying to hold on
but I can't let him
I gotta let go
I gotta love
a man

He's Not Worth It

Have you ever had one of your sister friends call you up crying so hard you can barely understand what she's saying? And as you stop what you are doing and sit down, you instantly know that those types of tears only come from one source; a bad relationship. So many women, including myself, have cried needless tears over some guy that was not worth one-quarter of one drop of our tears. Yet at many times in our lives we either find ourselves making that heart wrenching phone call or being on the receiving end of one.

The power of receiving that phone call is that we are not emotionally connected to the man. We can see clearly that dude is not even worth the cost of the phone call. We know fully that he doesn't deserve our friend and she definitely doesn't deserve the drama he has brought into her world. But how do you tell your friend the truth when her heart is breaking and all she really wants is confirmation that everything is going to be all right? It depends on how you tell her that everything is going to be all right.

Every woman will not instantly end a relationship that is damaging her emotionally, or even physically. So when your sister friend calls you up and needs to vent, you should use that time wisely. Of course you may feel that girlfriend will not leave this man in this moment. You can still plant some grains of truth in her head.

You should remind her that sometimes the man we think is so wonderful really isn't. Tell her that sometimes in life we lose our minds over men other women would walk away from. Sometimes we're so busy believing a man is so great that we diminish our own light. We have to remember that we are worthy of better—better relationships, better love, and a better man.

The last thing any woman needs is a man who doesn't recognize and appreciate her greatness. Now I'm not saying that girlfriend may not have issues. Even if she has some issues, no one deserves to be mistreated or disrespected. So many times women hold onto relationships out of desperation or ego. I've talked with many women that stayed in deteriorating, unfulfilling, and loveless relationships because they simply did not want to start over and begin dating again.

Then there are women that are used to getting what they want from men and feel that a man is simply a challenge. They mistakenly think that they can either turn him into their dream man or win his heart. I've wasted my love and time in a relationship because of my ego. I know what it's like to want to win a man's heart just to see if you can be the first woman to make this man fall in love.

Let me share something with you. You cannot make anyone do anything they are not ready for or that they do not want to do. If a man's heart is not open to love then you cannot get him to fall in love with you. If a man says he is not ready to fall in love or that he's not ready for a relationship you will not be able to change his mind by being the best girlfriend to him. His mind and heart are already made up and you need to decide whether you want to invest your time or move on to a man that is ready for love.

If a man says that he just wants to be friends or just hang out, believe him and hear him clearly. So many sisters waste years and tears thinking that a man will change his mind because the so-called friendship has evolved from platonic to sexual. Unless the man specifically says he wants a relationship with you then do not assume that the friendship has morphed into a relationship. All you have created is a so-called friendship based around sex and filled with heartache for yourself.

It is essential that a relationship have balance. The bible gives us one of the most powerful lessons we can ever learn about love—be ye equally yoked. In addition to balance, it's essential that both partners feel that the timing is right.

If a man says he could fall for you but the timing is not right, or that he believes in love it's just not the right time or any thing that even closely mentions that the timing is not right for you to be in love or in a relationship, you need to realize quickly that the only thing you will always and forever have with this man is imbalance and eventually, if you fall in love with him, unhappiness.

In my opinion, the downfall of relationships occurred when we started believing that opposites attract. In some ways I know the energies that make you differ can seem exciting at first. But in order to have a lasting, fulfilling relationship there are certain things we must have in common with our partner.

I learned the difficult way that as an entrepreneur it was necessary for me to have a man that was also an entrepreneur. When one person believes that working in corporate America is the only way to be successful, while the other person views that as the ultimate nightmare of a life, the two are creating a relationship of imbalance. It is important that you share the same values as your man. It's essential that you share the same type of passion, focus, and love for something other than yourselves in life. I'm not saying, at all, that you have to have the same dream in life. I do believe that you should dream the same way. If you dream big then he should be able to dream big right along with you.

I've talked to so many women that share tales of struggle and working hard to accomplish their goals only to find themselves in a relationship with a man that is not hustling as hard as she has or would, or accomplished as much as she has. That, in essence, is settling. We deserve more.

If you are going to have a great relationship then you have to be in a relationship with a man that you think is great. You deserve a man that recognizes his greatness and sees and appreciates your greatness. When you focus on having the best relationship and only sharing your life with a man that you know is great then you alleviate the possibility that you will be calling up one of your sister friends wondering why and how you got into a devastating relationship.

If a man ever tells you that you just think you're better than him, or utters that you're not so great, you need to get away from him as soon as possible. This man is clearly telling you something. He's simply stating that he doesn't think you're that great. He doesn't think you're worthy of him. And if we break it down, perhaps you make him feel insecure. This is not a time to analyze what he's saying or ask him why he would say such a thing. You need to maintain your dignity and respect for yourself by choosing not to indulge in such a conversation and instead know clearly that any man that cannot see your greatness does not deserve you.

In order to get the loving relationship you really want, you have to be a loving person and you must know that you are worthy of amazing love and joyful relationships. Then if any man attempts to enter your world without being equally yoked with you, you can simply allow the wind to hit his feet so that he may get away from you quickly. No one needs or deserves drama and it is our responsibility to stop creating situations for drama. Choose the people you allow to be in your world wisely.

Lesson
We all deserve to be loved, adored and appreciated. If you do not feel these things for your partner than you should let them go so that you both can attract someone that can authentically reciprocate feelings of love, adoration and appreciation.

Do You Listen?

Men tell you what they want from you. When you say, "Where is this relation-ship going?" and he responds, "Let's just take it one day at a time." When you ask to define the relationship, and he says, "Why do we need a definition?" When you express your great affection for the man, and he says, "That's great, you're very special." When he says I love you when you're being intimate but cannot utter the words at any other time. When he doesn't attempt to get to know your friends or become very involved in your life. When he never calls you his girl-friend but constantly refers to you as his friend, even though you've been inti-mate, then this man is speaking to you and showing you through his actions that you are not his queen. You are somebody for the moment-somebody to sleep with, somebody to watch a movie with, and somebody to spend idle time with until another woman comes along.

The questions are: Are you comfortable with what he's saying to you? Are you satisfied with the type of relationship you have with him? Do you only want him around for the moment?

To answer those questions you have to know exactly where you are in your life and compare it to the life place this man is in.

If you are comfortable with a man that regards you as a special, sweet woman rather than the love of his life then you need to realize that you are a lower prior-ity in his life. If you believe that his inability to define the relationship after months of dating is simply because he needs more time to get to know you, then you will perpetually be in wonderment of where the relationship is headed until you realize that it's only going where it already is.

A man knows what he wants and men are actually much more honest about it then we give them credit for. A man will tell you how he feels about you through his actions. Some men will even tell you that they're not ready for a commitment or anything serious right now. Some men may tell you that their last relationship changed their perspective on women so they are taking it slow for a while. And rather than making a wise decision and leaving the man alone when we hear all that, women interpret his honest action or communication in a totally different way.

When a man clearly tells you that he is not ready for a commitment or anything serious right now and you decide, "He doesn't know me well enough yet, because then he'll surely change his mind," you are deluding yourself. When a man says he's taking it slow with future relationships because the last relationship ended poorly, you need to realize that his time line for healing and your time line for making this a committed relationship are two entirely different things. Sisters, we have to digest one truth into our being—you can only get what someone is willing to give. Love cannot be bargained for or contemplated.

In order to have a loving relationship both you and the man have to be willing to embrace love. You both have to have open hearts and minds. You must both be healed and empowered from previous relationships. You must both be willing to regard one another as unique individuals. You must both be willing to trust fully, even if your heart was ripped to shreds in a prior relationship. You must both be willing to believe in the power of love and the importance of friendship prior to entering into a relationship. You must both be in the same life place. Life place is so important. Job title or financial resources do not define life place. Spiritual outlooks, values, political views, goals and philosophy of life determine life place.

I firmly believe that women must stop denying what they really want in a relationship just to have a semblance of a relationship. In essence we must stop dealing with men simply because we do not want to be alone. If we want a monogamous relationship then we must honor the relationship of others and only date men that want the same thing. If we want a committed relationship then we must be honest with ourselves and with the men we're dating.

When a man says he's not ready for anything serious right now but we know in our hearts that we're tired of the dating scene and would really like to be with one man, then we need to honor our truth. We as women have to be willing to keep it moving. Maybe this man in front of you is not going to be the love of your life but if he's telling you clearly what he wants, be clear about what you want and you two can depart as associates now, maybe even become friends, and perhaps spare your heart some pain and your life some drama if you are honest about what you want.

So many women hear a man say he's not ready and keep dating him like he's suddenly going to change his mind. Are we insane or hard of hearing? Do we listen when a man tells us what he wants? Sister the most empowering place to be is when you hear a man clearly and you make the best decision for yourself in that moment. Give yourself what you need and stop just meeting his needs. Many times when a man has made it clear that he's going to be less than available to us we'll continue to make ourselves available to him.

We're going to do something powerful right now. We're going to take responsibility for our relationships. We're going to voice our opinions about what we want and expect. We're not going to think about scaring a man away because we state that we want to get married in the future. Any man that gets frightened because you say you want to get married one day has some clear ego or relationship issues. First of all, you're not saying you want him to jump up and marry you. You're definitely not saying he's the prince that you've been waiting for all your life and you must marry him. So he clearly has some of his own issues to deal with.

I want you to do something for yourself from this day forward. If a man gets turned off because you share the vision of your future with him, which includes getting married, then let him go. Do not play down what you want or dismiss your vision because he doesn't want the same things. Empower yourself by letting the man go forward in his life. Stop wasting your time and energy trying to change a man's mind. Stay focused on your needs and expectations and only date men that can meet those needs and expectations.

If it is our hope to get married then we must choose men that want the same thing. If we want to have a close relationship with God then we must select men that want the same thing so that our focus never goes away from God, it just expands to include our man. If we want a good man then we must start believing that they exist and stop listening to the women that say men aren't any good. If we want a spiritual connection and loving relationship with a man, but we've never seen a good example of that type of relationship, we must trust in our ability to create greatness in the world.

God placed you here as a blessing to the world and as co-creator of your life. Therefore you have the ability to create things that do not exist, to create those things that no one has ever seen before and to defy the expectations of others and yourself by becoming the very example you had hoped and prayed for. You can become a woman that other women look up to in admiration. You can become part of that powerful couple that has an amazing relationship. You simply have to choose better relationships and better men. You have to make wise decisions and listen to your heart and intuition.

Lesson

Relationships require honesty. Be honest about what you want and expect from a relationship and then enter relationships with someone that demonstrates through words and actions that they want and expect the same thing.

Are You Under the Influence?

Do you recall those days when you felt absolutely drained? You felt lethargic, overwhelmed and so *out of it?* You felt as though your energy was being pulled in so many directions that it was difficult for you to keep everything in balance? You get to the point where you say, if one more person asks me one more thing that will be it?

I know we all can have those types of days. Some folks live their entire lives in that terrible state of imbalance. But I'd like to share something with you. The feelings of anxiety, being overwhelmed and stressed are all choices. We have control over the stress in our lives. And we have the ability to keep our lives in balance. How? Stress is controlled by whom you allow into your life, how willing you are to tell your own truth, and how much courage you have to live up to and stand up for your truth. Do you have the courage to be honest? Do you have the ability to say no to someone when you simply do not have the time or positive energy to give them? Do you know how to give yourself time to rest and be replenished?

Let me clearly tell you that it is as simple as it sounds. If you want to feel in control of your life then you must take control. If you want less stress in your life then you must determine who is worthy of being in your life and how much time you will allow yourself to spend with people that drain your energy. Many times it is our family members, job or children putting a drain on us, and we mistakenly believe that there is no way to regain balance in dealing with them. Unfortunately we believe that we must give our energy to anyone and everyone when they need us. It is simply not so.

We have been conditioned, particularly as women, to give more than we receive. People have told us the wonderful belief that it is better to give than to receive. Yeah, well when you're giving way more than you're receiving and you can feel that your energy is depleted then you have become imbalanced and you need to become the receiver at this moment. So in the case of family members, job or children you must consciously choose to create balance. We must choose to give ourselves what we need and understand that we have far greater control of our life and our energy than we realize.

There are times when my girls are driving me nuts by asking me as many questions as there are answers in the Jeopardy game vault. The phone is ringing. People want articles. I have deadlines. A site to maintain. A relationship to nourish and appreciate. And then times can arise when it all becomes a bit much and I have to put it back in balance. Many times it can simply mean shutting my door and allowing the girls to be. The idea that they may make a complete mess in the house doesn't mean nearly as much when I know I need to regain my emotional balance. The beauty of control in your life is knowing when to use it and when to release it.

Yes, your family members, job or children only overwhelm you at times because you ALLOW them too. If you simply relinquished a bit of control—left work early to live your life, taught your children to appreciate their own 'me time,' and allowed the phone to go to voice mail at times, you wouldn't be so stressed, anxious, drained and overwhelmed.

We are human so there will be times when we feel lethargic, overwhelmed and so *out of it*. But we are spirits also and therefore we have the power to create a better life for ourselves each and every day, in every moment.

We must stop going under the influence of others who bring negative energy, drama and stress. We must learn how to make the best choices for our spiritual, emotional and mental well-being.

I know for sure that when you commit to living a life you love then you instantly make a commitment to choose what is best for your life and your spirit. You make a decision to keep your life and world in balance. You choose to look at life with eyes of love rather than judgment.

You choose to create peace in your home, your work and your life by every choice you make.

So the next time you feel lethargic, overwhelmed and so *out of it* make a conscious choice to get back into your life and make the best decision for yourself in this moment.

Lesson
We can either become overwhelmed by our emotions and stay in a pattern of constantly reacting to and being affected by others. Or we can remember that emotions are something we can control and therefore we participate in life without becoming imbalanced or overextended.

Before I Do

a first vow
when you look at me
look at me with honesty
let me always see your truth
show me your spirit

a second vow
is to always be
a part of your growth
I want to see your spiritual evolution

a third vow
is to treat you
as you treat me
with respect
love
sincerity
compassion
my vow is to love you
as you love me
      free

One Partner, No Dependents

A young woman was telling me how wonderful her new boyfriend was and the commitment he had to making sure their relationship remained positive and led to marriage. He created a financial and life plan that incorporated her into his life in many ways. He assured that her financial and emotional needs were met. He listened and supported her emotionally in her business pursuits. He sounded wonderful for her. My question was what do you do?

She hadn't mentioned doing anything for him. She hadn't made a life plan or financial plan for herself. She hadn't started saving her money so that she could contribute to the home they wanted to buy in the future. He was working two jobs, starting a business and saving his money to help fund his business as well as her future business. And she was shopping in the mall or telling him she thought everything he was doing was wonderful.

I understand that as women we have a desire to feel loved, protected and supported. My only question, in this situation, is what are you bringing to the relationship? What makes you a partner in this relationship? If we truly believe in the power of partnership than we have to be honest with one another and ourselves and realize that it is essential that every relationship be equally yoked. If he's saving and you're spending, how are you working together? If he's making a life plan that includes you in his life as his wife and mother of his children and you're just sitting back to see if he messes up this relationship, how are you bringing positive energy to the relationship?

She didn't feel as though she was bringing anything to the relationship. She felt as though her boyfriend was doing everything to make the relationship work and she was more or less benefiting from his efforts. Well, of course her intuition was right and I told her it was essential to start making changes immediately while she was the only one noticing the imbalance in the relationship.

I can hear people pulling out their bibles now and saying that when a man finds a wife he finds a good thing. Uh huh, and do you think he will choose the woman that helped him in life or the one that just sat there and watched as he did everything? You see, in the beginning it may feel nice to a man's ego that you need him to do things for you. But there's a fine line between him doing things for you and you needing him to do everything for you and when he notices that difference you will no longer be seen as a wonderful part of his life. You'll be seen as a burden not a partner.

Lesson
Be the partner that you want and expect your man to be to you.

A Day of Realization

I remember when a friendship, which I once thought was dear, was ending. Isn't it amazing how the truth can stare us so boldly in the face yet we refuse to look directly at it? Instead, we make excuses for situations and attempt to justify someone's negative behavior? It took me awhile to realize that this woman I once regarded as a sister friend had slipped into the associate slot.

Although I was attempting to make our friendship still feel like family she was simply caught up in her own world. I would call her for small chitchat, try to make arrangements for lunch or dinner and email her just to ask her about her day. But, just as you know when the thrill is gone from a relationship, you know when it's gone from a friendship as well.

Aside from the times when we may have disagreements and arguments and know that we have to let our friend know how much they mean to us, we have to be mindful of how much energy we invest in saving a friendship when only one person is working toward saving it.

Our sister friends can become like family to us but we have to know when to stop trying so hard to be a friend. Just as we are worthy of wonderful love and blessings, we are also worthy of beautiful friendships.

Do not allow anyone to give you less than the best of themselves. You deserve a friend that cherishes your time, loves you like family, communicates with you when she's upset, and can laugh, cry and rejoice with you.

As I continue to move forward on the path God has set for me, I notice that there are some people that haven't been around as much since he started blessing me. There are some folks that started being around a little too much. Then there are some people who haven't changed a bit and still love and laugh with me in the same wonderful way.

Friendships evolve. Some people may be in your life until the day you die. Some people may only be in your life during a moment of your life. Whatever role someone plays, allow them to play that role and stop trying to make more out of a friendship than it really is. As T.D. Jakes once said, "If someone can walk out of your life, then let them walk." And I add to that, may the wind be beneath their feet so they can move quickly and new relationships can enter your world.

Of course there are times when there is just a lot going on in your friend's world and you should be considerate. But I'm not focusing on those times. I'm talking about the moments of a friendship when you can absolutely feel and your intuition is telling you that the friendship is deteriorating and you're the only one concerned about that. That's when you must know whether it is best to try to make it better or whether it's time to let it go.

Lesson
Friendships are evolving relationships. We will never know how long we will be friends with someone or how deep the friendship will become. But we can determine how much love, time, and energy we give to our friends.

When Love Calls

I was chatting with a friend when my call waiting beeped. When I clicked over I heard the voice of an aunt I hadn't seen in years telling me that my grandfather, my Pop Pop, was in the hospital and that I should give him a call. I jotted down the name of the hospital, his room number and the telephone number at the hospital. As I lapsed back into conversation with my sister friend I quickly forgot about making that important phone call. When I finally stopped laughing and chatting I glanced at the clock. Due to the late hour I told myself I would have to call Pop Pop in the morning and I went to bed.

I woke up in the morning, went to high school and found out the moment I arrived home that Pop Pop had died in the wee hours of the morning. From that moment in my life I vowed to always share my feelings. I learned the importance of telling someone you love him or her when they need to hear it, not just when you're comfortable in saying it.

So many people have been hurt in prior relationships and are dealing with emotional pain and trust issues that they simply have lost the ability to be vulnerable and trust in the power of God's love.

So many of us feel love in our heart far long before we speak it to the person we love. The unfortunate thing about humans is that we take our time for granted. We assume we will get to share our feelings or show our kindness at some time in the future. But who granted you tomorrow? All we ever have is today and so we must have the courage to live today fully. We must have the confidence to tell others how we genuinely feel about them in this moment. We must have the courage to show someone how much they mean to us in this moment.

Although we may have been hurt before or had our heart broken, we must trust that eventually true love is going to come into our lives and we must trust that the relationship could contain everything that we have hoped, wished and prayed for.

A simple lesson I have learned is that love happens. Love happens when, where and with whom it wants. Love is not concerned with your fear of giving your heart away. Love is not concerned with your fear of being vulnerable and trusting another person. There is a great disco song that essentially says when love calls you better answer, don't let it slip away, it may never come again.

My Pop Pop taught me a lesson in his passing that I share with you, be there for those you love and be ready to love at anytime. So now when I get a call that a loved one is sick or a friend is having a terrible day, I take the call. I show up for my friends' lives not just when it's convenient for me but when they need me to be there.

When romantic love began to appear in my life I was nearly scared away but I knew that my trust in God would always help me with any love I have for a man. I know for sure that if you have God in your heart and life, then you can never be afraid to love and if you are ever afraid to love then you have not fully experienced God. God is love and love is God and God shows up when you need him so do the same for those you claim to love—show up and show your love.

Lesson
Love is not an experience that is written in your appointment book as a "To Do." Love happens each and everyday. If we would get over our own fear, vulnerability and insecurities and simply allow ourselves to feel and give love, we would experience love on much deeper levels.

"Love has its own time, its own season, and its own reasons for coming and going. You cannot bribe it or coerce it or reason it into staying. You can only embrace it when it arrives and give it away when it comes to you."

—Kent Nerburn

Love

Unknowingly
I have searched for you
longed so deeply for you
that I tried to grab you
from the soul of another
just to feel your glow
and give my will to your power
I have cast my hope of you
upon another
and saw my desire for you
through their eyes

I have longed for you so much
that I have pretended you existed
created illusions of you with another
imagined I was experiencing
the breathtaking embrace
only you can give
I have learned along the way
that I cannot conjure you up
like some magical brew
I cannot make another being want to
succumb to you
The only way I can have you
is to be open to you
and to be near someone
who is open to you as well

I prayed for the moment
to experience your grace
to feel your wave

overpower me
authenticate me
and make me feel you
within my heart
within my soul
within every cell of my being

I no longer sit and wait
pray and gaze
read and wonder

about you
Instead I feel you in my life
and I thank you
for showing up
and exuding through
such a strong man

All my life I searched for you
and the moment I gave up
is the moment you took hold
and showed me
that you exist
have always been present
and are quite real
I embrace you
I welcome you
and I hope you stay
  forever

Choices

"This person doesn't really fit the model of what people expect of me. He doesn't have the look I would normally go for. How do you know if someone is your type?" These were the questions that popped into my email from a reader. So, I took a moment to give it some thought. My spirit told me the greatest injustice we can do to our spirit and mental well-being is to live any form of our life solely based on the expectations of others. It is so true that family, friends, co-workers, and even strangers, expect something from us based on our look, our talk, our walk, our ambitions, and our essence.

We have to be mindful that we are in pursuit of authenticity, peace of mind, happiness and love. In order to receive those things we must be willing to step out of the norm and live for ourselves. In the end what will matter is whether we were happy, fulfilled and loved. What will matter is if we feel we made the right choice for ourselves.

Though someone may love you dearly they cannot govern the needs of your heart or spirit. No one can fulfill you or make you happy. You have to fulfill yourself and make yourself happy.

So if a man does not meet the definition of a type you would be with, according to your friends and family, you must truly ask yourself—who am I trying to please?

Our priority must be our happiness. In the end, a person that loves you will be there with you through your choices. Happiness is something we must choose to experience. And the one way we can get on the path to happiness is by not using the expectations of others to make the decisions for our lives.

Lesson
Live for yourself not for what others will think of or expect of you.

Step Five—Allow Your Love to Change The World

○ ○

We all learn to love, in some way, in our lifetime. Hopefully we will master the first skill, which is love of self. Then the second skill, which is loving someone else as much as you love yourself. And the third and final step, which we should strive for before leaving this earth, is to love your human family. Understand that you are a precious part of the universe. You are essential to the world community. Embrace that fact and then allow your love to change the world—by being authentically you, by treating others with love, and by giving your positive energy, in some way, to something that makes the world a better place for generations to come.

If I speak in the tongues of men and of angels, but have not love, I am only a resounding gong or a clanging cymbal. If I have the gift of prophecy and can fathom all mysteries and all knowledge, and if I have a faith that can move mountains, but have not love, I am nothing. If I give all I possess to the poor and surrender my body to the flames, but have not love I gain nothing. Love is patient, love is kind. It does not envy, it does not boast, it is not proud. It is not rude, it is not self-seeking, it is not easily angered, it keeps no record of wrongs. Love does not delight in evil but rejoices with the truth. It always protects, always trusts, always perseveres. Love never fails.

—1 Corinthians 13:1-8

My Breath

at times
you were at one
with my breath
an essential part of me
giving life to me
sustaining me
with that euphoric feeling

at times
you were at one
with my breath
and I loved you as me

at times
you were beautiful
an essential part of me
and I loved you as me

at times you are my voice
you say the words
that are in my heart

you give authority
to that part of me
that acknowledges
that love is a necessity

at times I love you
as if you are me
you exude that confidence
that sweet sexy smile

that makes me remember
that once
you were an essential part of me
and I loved you as me
and I loved you as me
and I loved you as me

the only way
to regain my breath
is to love you as me
again

The Power of Love

Love is an exhilarating feeling. It reminds you of the speed of a roller coaster, the lull of sitting on the deck of a cruise ship, and the moment when you laugh so hard you have to hold your stomach. Love can give you so many wonderful emotions that everyone should experience being in love and falling in love at least once in their life.

Someone once said that it is better to have loved and lost than to have never loved at all. If you've never loved deeply than you will think that quote is pure gibberish. But once you have loved and you can conjure up the memories of someone smiling at you with love, sharing a secret laugh with you or just sitting together in silence and feeling totally comfortable, then you will read that quote in agreement.

Of course no human being is perfect therefore no relationship is perfect. But love should have more perfect moments than not. A loving relationship should have many moments that make you feel like the most blessed person in the world. Love should make you feel as though you can accomplish any goal you set your mind upon. Love should make you feel beautiful, loved and adored. Love should make you feel as though someone loves you and delights in seeing you walk into a room. Love should let you know that your smile makes someone's day and your laugh can cure someone's pain. Love should teach you about yourself, expand who you are as a woman, and show you how much love you are capable of giving to another person. Love should help you to feel strong.

Although you will have moments when you're afraid to be so vulnerable to another person, the love you have for them will ease your mind and allow your heart to continue to be open and loving toward that person. Once we learn that vulnerability lasts only for a moment we will allow ourselves to go to deeper levels in our relationship. In a trusting and loving relationship, the man will feel just as vulnerable. He will also be just as willing as you are to keep loving through his fear of letting go of himself completely in order to fully share his heart with you.

An equally balanced, loving relationship is one of the most beautiful experiences we can have in this life. We should treasure every moment of it and never take a loving moment for granted. Once you allow the love in your heart and soul to be given to another person freely you will liberate yourself and see them with love.

God brought this man into your life for a reason. It could be to learn a lesson or to learn several lessons. But once you trust the experience, love, as God loves you, and feel the spirit of a man and know whether he has good or bad intentions you will be in a more powerful position and enter into relationships that appear better for you. Although we'll never know how a relationship will turn out, we can always trust our intuition to tell us how we should deal with a man. So, let's trust ourselves and trust the power of love.

Love transforms. Love is glorious. Love is the most amazing feeling we can experience. Even when your issues or insecurities want to get the best of you, remember the power of love. Remember how wonderful love feels. Tune into the moment when you're standing in church and swaying, hearing a good word or reading something that truly touches your spirit. Can you feel that moment? Well love will feel like that if you allow yourself to sink into it and enjoy.

Lesson
Love expands who you are. Human beings should be able to tap into their spirit and feel an amazing sense of love for themselves. The best gift of life is knowing that you are loved, because you love yourself. Then you will know how to give and experience love with someone else.

The Glory of Love

Opening your heart to love
is a scary thing
putting your heart on the line
has never been easy
it takes courage to open your heart
and get to know someone
and allow them to know you well

it's so easy to keep up that wall
and hold back all the fears
thoughts of pain
      but what about the other side
what about tender kisses
looking into that someone's eyes
and knowing this person loves me
there's no better feeling in the world
      remember
it's not so bad

don't you want to laugh

hold hands
love and be loved
again

life is all about chance
every man and woman deserves one
so disregard
slowly if you like
your thoughts of pain
and open up
to the glory of love

My Inspiration

My soul mission in life is to empower women to make better choices. It sounds so simple but when it's your life work, it's very personal. That's why the news story of a young woman in Atlanta really affected me. A young woman, just 17 years old, was killed by her boyfriend and discarded, as if she were garbage, in a nearby field. I thought about this young woman and realized that we are all accountable for that. Not her death, but her life. A young woman, just 17 years old, died because of domestic violence. This young woman also left three children behind. Did I mention she was just 17 years old?

Who stepped in to help her or the thousands of other young women that desperately need a mentor? Who helps the young women and men who need to see a face of strength, courage and love to show them that there are options in life? Who helps these young women and men find a way to live extraordinary lives rather than merely existing in mediocrity and poverty? Where are we? How can we continue to live our lives as if we are not all connected? How can we continue to go on without stepping in to make someone's life better?

Our soul purpose is to make an individual effort to make this world a better place and each individual will help to make a collective difference. But when we forget our soul purpose and think that nothing can be done, then we receive the overwhelming rate of teenage pregnancies and murders. Then we have escalating high school dropouts and more young men in prison then in college. We have to do better. The world deserves better. God expects us to do better than this.

How did a young woman, just 17 years old, die nearly in front of her home and leave three children behind? We must never get to a place when the news of such incidents no longer shocks and outrages us. We are children of God and based on that fact alone we are accountable for our family, the entire human family.

We have to take time to get over ourselves enough that we can reach out and help someone else. We have to realize that the world exists and thrives based on the talents and precious spirits that God pours into the earth. You must stop blocking your blessings and talents now. You never know who needs to hear your words, see your art, hear you sing, or use your invention.

You are here for a purpose, and your very existence requires that you live your purpose. And if you keep hemming and hawing, waiting for the right time, waiting for signs, or living in fear or with obstacles and limitations, then you will block your blessings and you just may block someone else's blessings as well.

Let's stop making so many excuses. Let's really get down to the truth of life and remember the simple things: Treat people as you would want to be treated; Live in love; Live your purpose; Never take your moments for granted; Reach out and help another person to live better, even if it's just to make them laugh, or to be an ear when they really need someone to talk too.

Realize that you are never alone in this life. We are all connected. Your joy is my joy. My pain is your pain. Your triumph is my triumph. The world can only be changed one person at a time. Let's make a commitment to do our part. Let's do more than we thought we could and more than others would expect. Give your best self to this world. Someone, somewhere, needs your spirit.

Lesson
Your purpose in life is to make the world a better place in your own way.

"If one has not given everything, one has given nothing."

—Georges Guynemer

You Are A Dreamer

In one of my favorite childhood movies, Willy Wonka gets this glazed look in his eyes and says something like, "We are the dreamers of dreams. We are the dream makers," and then he bursts into song. Everyone looked at him like he was crazy but those lines always stuck with me.

We are the dreamers of dreams. We are the dream makers. Even when I was young those two sentences told me two things—you can dream and you can create. We are all given the gift of creation. We all have created the lives we're living now through our thoughts and actions. Along the way all of our choices have added up and placed us exactly where we are now.

One of the keys to creating a life you love and living your dream is that you never change who you are at your core. No matter how many obstacles you endure and challenges you face, never allow life to block your spirit from shining out into the world. Never let things get so overwhelming that you no longer dream of a better life. Our goal should be to dream and to make our dreams a reality.

I encourage you to make your dreams manifest because you are destined to do it. I know that God talks to us all. God attempts to reach and touch the lives of us all. We just have to be ready for the word. We have to realize when it is our time to shine and live fully.

We are more powerful than we realize. We are more blessed than we recognize. We are more talented than we give ourselves credit for. We are strong and we are capable of changing the world. It's all about perspective. Let's make our dreams a reality.

I hope that you love as though you have never been hurt, dream bigger today than you did yesterday, and know that your spirit has the strength to endure all of life's trials and triumph over all painful moments. If you want to make your wishes come true and experience the best love of your life, you must make those dreams come true. You are a dream maker.

Lesson
The only person that can ever block you from experiencing love is you.

"Love is the greatest gift that one generation can leave to another."

—Richard Garnett

Your Daily Words of Power

Everyday I want you to say these powerful statements aloud to tap into the love that exists within you.

- I am a genius.
- I am powerful.
- I am perfect in the eyes of God.
- I am deeply loved and I am worthy of love.
- I am beautiful and intelligent.
- I am phenomenal.
- I have the power of God in my body.
- I love, believe and trust myself.
- I am creating a life I love and the only person that can block me from living the life of my dreams is me.
- I choose a life filled with success, love, peace, joy, wealth and great health.

Love Lessons

The List

1. You are responsible for your happiness and mental freedom.

2. You deserve all the love, peace, wealth and happiness God can bring into your life and to truly receive those blessings, you will have to choose to forgive yourself and others.

3. As long as we are on this earth we have the ability to choose a life of happiness, no matter what we may have endured in our past.

4. Never take your moments for granted.

5. Do more than you think you can and more than others expect. Your spirit is needed to help save the world.

6. Life can and will change the moment you decide to take control of it.

7. You decide how long and whether the negative words or behavior of a person will affect your life and relationships.

8. The only way to obtain happiness and really love your life is to put yourself first.

9. We are blessed to be able to talk about the challenges in our lives, because if we trust the process, our talk will soon turn to how we overcame it all.

10. God is not meant to just get us through the bad times. Our God can take us to the powerful, happy times where we're smiling from our soul, loving our life, laughing and loving who we are and how we are.

11. Live as though God wanted you to enjoy every moment.

12. If someone attempts to steal your joy you must combat him or her with your positive energy. If someone attempts to 'bring you down a peg' you must remind yourself of the great steps you have taken. If someone

wants to only see you as the person you were in the past, you must claim who you are today and get away from that energy.

13. No matter what you go through in life, you can either come through it broken or you can come through it with renewed energy and strength. It's your choice.

14. Be thankful for all that God has done and will do for you.

15. The love we have for ourselves must exude through our being and reflect into our lives.

16. The key to finding love is to love and honor yourself first—every part of you.

17. Acknowledge the greatness that resides within you.

18. There are some choices that we cannot change and inevitably they will change us. We can then do one of two things, we can live a life of pity, and shame and regret or we can heal our hearts and spirits, acknowledge the pain and free ourselves from the drama.

19. When you tell yourself everyday to live a life you love, you will create circumstances to make that a reality.

20. You deserve to be appreciated for all that you do and you should appreciate what others do for you.

21. Even during your most difficult moment you can maintain control of your life by staying in control of your emotions.

22. With God in your life you will always have more than enough to get through the difficult times of your life.

23. Sometimes not getting what you prayed for is a blessing.

24. The characteristic that makes you attractive is the loving spirit you have and the way you share and show that love with others.

25. Your intuition will always give you the right answers for your life situations; you just have to be willing to listen.

26. Have relationships in which your intelligence, heart and standards are respected, appreciated and honored.

27. We deserve honest, loving relationships and the only way to get that is to be honest and loving.

28. We must take responsibility for the relationships we enter into and the men we bring into our lives.

29. Every man tells you how he feels about you.

30. We must be clear about what we want, need and expect from a relationship in the very beginning and we have to be very honest with ourselves and our potential partner about those things.

31. Open and honest communication is essential to all of our relationships in life.

32. We have to be sure to see people the way they genuinely are rather than how we wish or believe them to be as individuals.

33. If you really want the world to be better, the best place to start is with yourself.

34. We must never forfeit who we are at our core in order to make someone else feel happy and fulfilled

35. Life is not about changing who you are in order to have love. Life is about being exactly who your spirit says you should be and attracting love to you.

36. Set standards for yourself and know the difference between sacrifice and compromise.

37. Sometimes you have to walk away from someone you love in order to have the freedom and happiness you seek.

38. Seeking revenge on a person simply wastes your time and energy. The best revenge you will ever have is to live the best life and be the best person you can.

39. You can only have the best life has to offer when you refuse to settle or become complacent and you choose to become accountable for all aspects of your life.

40. Even if a man is a good person, it doesn't mean he is good for you.

41. We have to be willing to let go of the mediocre things in our life and go toward the greatness God has waiting for us.

42. In order to have all the love you deserve you must expect love to manifest in your life.

43. Every relationship you enter into defines who you are and makes a statement about you to the world.

44. If you want to love your life then you must take action every day to love the life you live.

45. In order to have the loving relationship that you want, you must honor the relationships of others.

46. If you want the best life and relationship God can offer you then you must only expect and accept the best.

47. There is a tremendous difference between what your insecurities tell you and what your intuition shares with you and you must learn to know the difference.

48. You decide how long and whether the negative words or behavior of a person will affect your life and relationships.

49. The life you really want is waiting for you. You just have to accept everything that it entails—the work, the process, the spiritual journey, the elimination of some friends, the true dependence on God, the belief that you are blessed, the knowledge that greatness is within you, and the commitment to do what you were sent here to do.

50. If we would just take the time to get to know one another, and trust our intuition, we could save ourselves from dealing with a lot of drama and heartache.

51. We are all capable of creating what we need to have a fulfilling life.

52. Your expectations can limit or free you in life and love.

53. God brings a person or situation into our lives to test, bless or teach us about ourselves.

54. We can only receive what we already believe we deserve and are going to get.

55. Faith is not selective. If you believe in the power of God then you trust that God can work in your life in all ways.

56. A person will only treat you the way you allow her or him to treat you.

57. We can block our own greatness because we do not acknowledge that just as we had a choice in the past, we now have a choice in our future.

58. The moment you know that your happiness matters more than the opinions of others, you will change your life.

59. We all have the ability to look into the eyes of a person and see their spirit, we simply have to trust and honor our first thought about the person.

60. The last thing any woman needs is a man who doesn't recognize and appreciate her greatness.

61. God shows up when you need him, so do the same for those you claim to love—show up and show your love.

62. No one needs or deserves drama and it is our responsibility to stop creating situations for drama.

63. If you are going to have a great relationship then you have to be in a relationship with a man that you think is great. You deserve a man that recognizes his greatness and sees and appreciates your greatness.

64. In order to have a loving relationship both you and the man have to be willing to embrace love.

65. Women must stop denying what they really want in a relationship just to have a semblance of a relationship. In essence we must stop dealing with men simply because we do not want to be alone.

66. God placed you here as a blessing to the world and as co-creator of your life. Therefore you have the ability to create things that do not exist, to create those things that no one has ever seen before and to defy the expectations of others and yourself by becoming the very example you had hoped and prayed for.

67. Relationships, of all kinds, should be equally yoked.

68. Be the partner that you want and expect your man to be to you.

69. Friendships evolve. Some people may be in your life until the day you die. Some people may only be in your life during a moment of your life. Whatever role someone plays, allow them to play that role and stop trying to make more out of a friendship than it really is.

70. The greatest injustice we can do to our spirit and mental well being is living any form of our life solely based on the expectations of others.

71. Love should teach you about yourself, expand who you are as a woman, and show you how much love you are capable of giving to another person.

72. You never know who needs to hear your words, see your art, hear you sing, or use your invention.

73. The moment you know that your happiness matters more than the opinions of others, you will change your life.

74. No matter how many obstacles you endure and challenges you face, never allow life to block your spirit from shining out into the world.

75. Love as though you have never been hurt, dream bigger today than you did yesterday, and know that your spirit has the strength to endure all of life's trials and triumph over all painful moments.

76. We must stop holding ourselves back from opportunities to show and share our love.

77. There can be times when the opinions and actions of others are affecting your ability to have love in your life. Everyday you are either choosing to let them block you or you are choosing to release yourself from them so that you can move toward love.

78. We can either become overwhelmed by our emotions and stay in a pattern of constantly reacting to and being affected by others. Or we can remember that emotions are something we can control and therefore we participate in life without becoming imbalanced or overextended.

79. You have time for whatever you choose to have time for.

80. You are what you believe and you are where you want to be.

81. If you settle in one area of your life then by definition you are settling. Either you are settling or you are not. There is no in—between.

82. Stress is controlled by whom you allow into your life, how willing you are to tell your own truth, and how much courage you have to live up to and stand up for your truth.

83. We must choose to give ourselves what we need and understand that we have far greater control of our life and our energy than we realize.